Designing Arguments
Invention, Organisation, Style

Sunita Anne Abraham

Dedicated to Mamma & Papa

Library of Congress Cataloguing data

Title: Designing Arguments
Subtitle: Invention, Organisation, Style
Author: Sunita Anne Abraham

viii + 139 pages
1. Persuasion (Linguistics)
2. Argument (Discourse)
3. Textbook

ISBN   978-981-07-2239-5

Cover design
Sunita Anne Abraham

Contents

Chapter 5 Organisation

Chapter 6 Style

Chapter 7 The big picture

List of Figures

Preface

Every day, people seek to influence their own and others' beliefs, attitudes and behaviour through a non-coercive process of communication, known as persuasion. The study of the possible and permissible means of persuasion in any given situation has traditionally been the domain of rhetoric. Within the Western tradition, the term *rhetoric* can be traced all the way back to the emergence of Greek democracy in the fifth century BC.

In his treatise on the subject, the Greek philosopher Aristotle distinguishes three genres of rhetoric — forensic, epideictic and deliberative — based on the communicative purpose and audience addressed in each; and, highlights means of inventing, organising and styling arguments, appropriate to each genre. From classical Greece and Rome, European interest in rhetoric continued to ebb and flow during the medieval and enlightenment periods.

In the twentieth century, rhetoric experienced a revival in America via the Scottish *belle lettrist* tradition, resulting in the establishment of departments of rhetoric and speech communication. The flames of this revival were partly fanned by the North American academic debate tradition and the incorporation of rhetoric into freshman composition courses.

This volume differs from most textbooks on argument in that it is not a *how to* manual. Most textbooks teach students how to argue better, using a normative approach in which students evaluate arguments in order to emulate the good and avoid the bad.

As a linguist, I take a more descriptive and analytical approach, my goal being to understand how the discourse of persuasion works. In this slim volume, I invite readers to observe rather than evaluate how rhetors adaptively employ the resources afforded by language to invent, organise and style their arguments in response to audiences and argument occasions.

The emphasis throughout is on hands-on learning, aimed at helping readers customise a portable rhetorical toolkit for analysing persuasion messages, paying close attention to the interplay between text, context and subtext. To this end, every chapter is interspersed with activities for individual and group work.

My approach is deliberately selective. My aim is not to drown readers in tidal waves of information but to synthesise ideas from contemporary linguistics and Aristotelian rhetoric so as to encourage independent exploration of how persuasion (including self-persuasion) works, across cultures, genres and media.

Acknowledgements

I'm indebted to Madalena Cruz-Ferreira for drawing my attention to a variety of howlers in the draft version of this text. Thanks to your eagle eye and generous feedback, Madalena, this volume goes out a much stronger version of itself.

I'm equally indebted to Ilyas Afiq Hasshim for detailed and constructive comments from a student's perspective.

To my friends Tomasina Oh, Robin Loon, Suganthi & Paul Daniel, and the Varghese family, thank you for being there for me.

To my Heavenly Father, I owe my love, my life, my all!

Chapter 1 Argument

Why do we argue — what do we not argue about?

How are argument, explanation and persuasion related?

How do descriptive and prescriptive approaches differ?

What three complementary perspectives has argument been studied from?

1.1 What do we mean by argument?

In any field of study, it's important to specify:

❖ the **object** of inquiry — what we're investigating

❖ the **method** of inquiry — how we will investigate what we're curious about

❖ the **goal** of inquiry — what we seek to achieve through our inquiry

Our **object of inquiry** is persuasion discourse. Broadly speaking, *discourse* refers to situated language use, i.e. language used in a specific context for a specific purpose. *Persuasion discourse* encompasses situated language use in a variety of media (print, broadcast and online) whose purpose is to influence our own and others' beliefs (ideas), attitudes (values) and behaviour (actions).

Our **method of inquiry** integrates Aristotelian rhetoric (see section 2.1) and contemporary linguistics. As a linguist, I envisage the anatomy of human discourse in terms of skin, muscle and bone, as depicted in Figure 1.1. Lexico-grammar represents the surface layer — a text's skin, so to speak. Coherence relations correspond to the connective, or muscle, layer between skin and bone; and rhetorical structure (the rhetorical moves employed to achieve the text's communicative purpose) represent the text's bone structure.

| Lexico-grammar SKIN | Coherence relations MUSCLE | Rhetorical structure BONE |

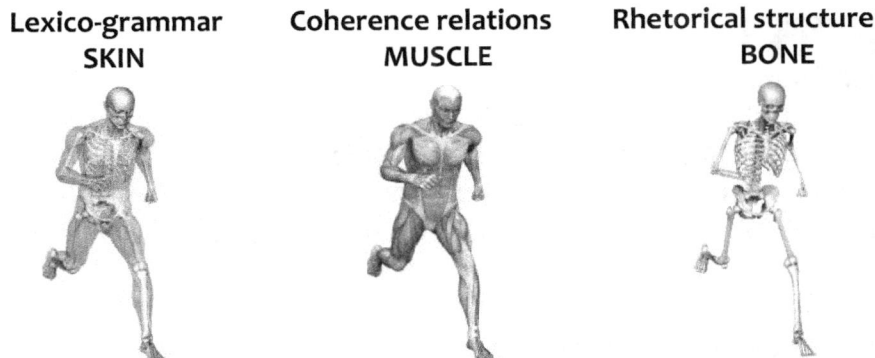

Figure 1.1   The skin, muscle and bone of discourse

The **goal** of our inquiry in turn is to understand how persuasion discourse works, i.e. how rhetors adaptively employ lexico-grammar, coherence relations and rhetorical structure to invent, organise and style arguments in response to specific audiences and situations.

Activity 1.1

What purposes can language serve? Think about all the activities you've engaged in today. Which ones involved language
❖ **centrally?**   (without language, these activities would be impossible)
❖ **peripherally?** (these activities require minimal language use)
❖ **not at all?**   (language is completely unnecessary for these activities)

Applied linguists have always been interested in the relationship between form and function. **Speech act theory** (see section 3.8) rests on the assumption that *saying is doing*. Some of the things we *do* with language include conveying information, maintaining social relationships, expressing feelings, and persuading ourselves as well as others.

In school, we're taught to read and write different genres, or text-types (see section 2.11), such as recounts, narratives, descriptions and explanations. Our main objective in this chapter is to understand the relationship between the genres labelled argument, explanation and persuasion. Figure 1.2 suggests three logical possibilities, i.e. that the three genres are unrelated, overlap or stand in a part-whole relationship.

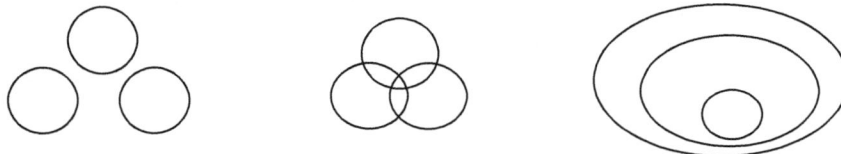

Figure 1.2   How are argument, explanation and persuasion related?

Activity 1.2

Step 1: Reflecting on the meaning of *argument*
What ideas and emotions does the word *argument* evoke? Has your understanding changed over time — what is your current understanding of *argument*? Do you think *argument* has more than one meaning? How does *argument* relate to *narration, description, explanation* and *persuasion*?

Step 2: Comparing definitions of *argument*
Look at several dictionaries (print or online) and talk to your friends so you can compare your understanding of *argument* with theirs. Feel free to modify your definition of *argument*, based on your dictionary search and discussion.

To find out how argument is perceived in different disciplines (note the assumption that there are different definitions of argument in different disciplines), university educators Phyllis Creme and Mary Lea asked postgraduate students, *What does 'argument' mean in your subject?* Here are the common themes that emerged in Creme and Lea's (2008, p.92-93) study:

- a piece of writing that is 'coherent' with its parts clearly connected to each other, in what many call a 'logical flow';
- the presentation of a case, or examining 'both sides' of a case;
- logically connected writing;
- a 'thesis with supporting evidence and reasons'

Step 3: Testing your definition of *argument*

Does your definition allow you to distinguish arguments from non-arguments in a reliable way? To test your definition, consider:

❖ Who argues with whom, when, where, how and why (for what purpose)?

❖ Is it worthwhile classifying arguments into different types — how would you do this, and why?

Like most words, the term *argument* is likely to conjure up different ideas and emotions in each of us. For some, an argument is a hostile communicative exchange involving raised voices and heated words as people try to score points off each other. This view of argument as verbal warfare is not altogether surprising, considering the many *argument-as-war* metaphors we use (see Lakoff and Johnson, 1981):

> *I'm going to demolish your argument.*

> *You have to attack their argument, point by point.*

> *She defended her position really well.*

Certainly, this notion of argument as an unpleasant adversarial exchange is one of the meanings listed in dictionaries. But, dictionaries also list a second meaning of *argument* as a reasoned presentation of ideas. This is the notion of argument that most argument textbooks discuss. Rhetorician Daniel O'Keefe (1976) refers to these two senses of *argument* as:

❖ **argument₁** (making an argument) and

❖ **argument₂** (having an argument), respectively.

O'Keefe's (1976) distinction between **argument₁** and **argument₂** is partly a response to rhetorician Wayne Brockriede's (1974) concept of argument. According to Brockriede (1974), argument is not something that exists out there in the real world, but a perspective that someone might adopt during a communicative exchange. In other words, a communicative activity does *not* constitute an *argument* until someone perceives what is happening as an argument.

O'Keefe's (1976) **argument₁** (assertions that people make for other people's acceptance) and **argument₂** (a type of interaction that people engage in) form the objects of inquiry for three complementary approaches to the study of argument (see section 1.6). As Thomas Hollihan and Kevin Baaske (2005) remark, most argument textbooks, including their own, focus on **argument₁** with the aim of helping students argue more logically. But, Hollihan and Baaske (2005) consider **argument₂** (argument as a communicative process of persuasion) to be equally important. As they put it, the "ability to conduct a civilized and polite argument with someone — the ability to argue and disagree with others while also managing to protect your relationship with them — is one of the most important things that people must learn" (p.6).

Learning how to argue productively is a skill that profoundly affects the quality of our interactions with others (Gottman, 1994). In completing Activity 1.2, you may have found yourself to be among the people who (have been taught to) believe that arguments are hazardous to healthy human relationships and that they should therefore be avoided at all costs. Indeed, as argument researchers Sally Jackson and Scott Jacobs (1980) remark, being labelled *argumentative* is not generally considered a compliment, since argumentative individuals are typically viewed as disagreeable, unpleasant or hostile.

The tendency to approach almost any issue in an aggressively adversarial way is what linguist Deborah Tannen (1998) dubs *the argument culture* in her book of the same title. But, Tannen is not advocating that people should stop arguing. Rather, what Tannen (1998, 2002) and other linguists like Diane Belcher (1997) take issue with is a toxic argument culture, pervaded by aggressive metaphors of war and symbolic slaying of one's adversaries where "criticism, attack, or opposition are the predominant if not the only ways of responding to people or ideas" (Tannen, 1998, p.7). Tannen's recommendation, crystallised in the subtitle of her book, is to move *from debate to dialogue*.

To clarify what an argument is (and isn't), let's consider an excerpt from *Monty Python's Flying Circus* (key in the phrase *Argument Clinic* to watch the entire six-minute sketch on YouTube). In this skit, a man approaches a reception desk and tells the receptionist that he would "like to have an argument, please". The receptionist directs the man to room 12A, where he starts interacting with the room's occupant, Mr Vibrating. Soon, however, the man informs Mr Vibrating that the activity in which they're engaged is not in fact argument but mere contradiction:

1	Man	*Look this isn't an argument.*
2	Mr Vibrating	*Yes it is.*
3	Man	*No, it isn't, it's just contradiction.*
4	Mr Vibrating	*No it isn't.*
5	Man	*Yes it is.*
6	Mr Vibrating	*It is not.*
7	Man	*It is. You just contradicted me.*

8	Mr Vibrating	*No I didn't.*
9	Man	*Ooh, you did!*
10	Mr Vibrating	*No, no, no, no, no.*
11	Man	*You did, just then.*
12	Mr Vibrating	*No, nonsense!*
13	Man	*Oh, look this is futile.*
14	Mr Vibrating	*No it isn't.*
15	Man	*I came here for a good argument.*
16	Mr Vibrating	*No you didn't, you came here for an argument.*
17	Man	*Well, an argument's not the same as contradiction.*
18	Mr Vibrating	*It can be.*
19	Man	*No it can't. An argument's a connected series of statements to establish a definite position.*
20	Mr Vibrating	*No it isn't.*
21	Man	*Yes, it is. It isn't just contradiction.*
22	Mr Vibrating	*Look, if I argue with you, I must take up a contrary position.*
23	Man	*But it isn't just saying 'No, it isn't'.*
24	Mr Vibrating	*Yes it is.*
25	Man	*No it isn't, argument is an intellectual process... contradiction is just the automatic gainsaying of anything the other person says.*
26	Mr Vibrating	*No it isn't.*
27	Man	*Yes it is.*
28	Mr Vibrating	*Not at all.*
29	Man	*Now, look! ....*

(Chapman *et al.*, 1999, pp.87-88)

What's made clear here is that argument involves more than the *Yes-No* tug-of-war of disagreement: *An argument's a connected series of statements to establish a definite position* (see speech turn 19 above). The example below should, I hope, clarify the difference between *disagreement* and *argument*.

A pair of siblings quarrelling

James	*You're mean and horrible!*
Jessica	*No, I'm not!*
James	*Yes, you are.*
Jessica	*No, I am NOT.*
Mother	*Stop arguing, you two!*
James	*Actually, Mum, we're not arguing. We're disagreeing.*

For now, let's use *an argument is a connected series of statements to establish a definite position* as our working definition of argument. In terms of structure, arguments comprise two parts linked by a process of reasoning (see Figure 1.3) — an assertion, or **claim**, which arguers want their audience to accept, and a connected series of statements functioning as **support** for this claim.

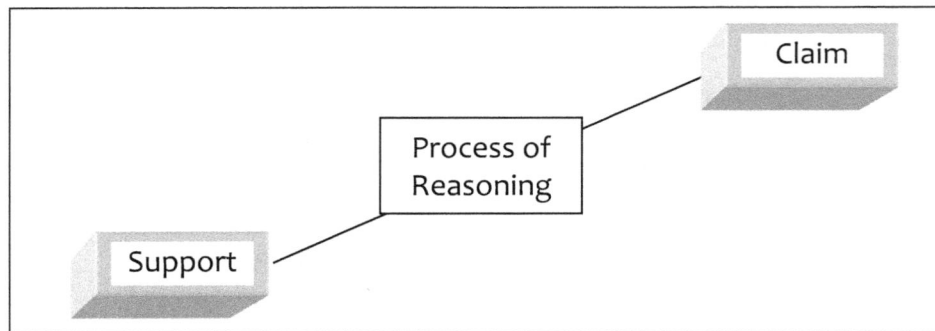

Figure 1.3   The structure of an argument

In terms of purpose, arguments seek to establish a definite position, influencing an audience's beliefs, attitudes and behaviour, based on the type of claim forwarded for the audience's acceptance (see sections 4.4 to 4.7 for more detail).

❖ **Truth claims** are assertions about what is or isn't the case, directed at influencing beliefs (ideas).

❖ **Value claims** are judgments of *good* and *bad*, directed at influencing an audience's attitudes (values).

❖ **Policy claims** are recommendations about what should or shouldn't be done, aimed at influencing behaviour (actions).

1.2   How are argument and explanation related?

To recap, arguments are communicative exchanges with an *X because Y* structure, where *X* is the claim proposed for the audience's acceptance and *Y* represents a connected series of statements supporting *X*. Structurally, arguments look very similar to explanations because both offer *reasons why*. For example, if you were late to class and your teacher asked you to explain your tardiness, you might say you were late *because* of a massive traffic jam along the campus ring road (*X because Y*). So, how can we distinguish argument from explanation? To answer that question, we need to consider communicative purpose, or why we argue.

Activity 1.3

Keeping in mind O'Keefe's (1976) distinction between **argument₁** and **argument₂**, jot down arguments that you've **made** and arguments that you've **had**. What were these arguments about, and what was your purpose in arguing? To whom did you **make** the argument? With whom did you **have** the argument? Did you achieve your purpose — how do you know whether you did or didn't?

All arguments emerge from disagreement, given our unique perspective on life, based on culture, education and experience, all of which colour our perceptions and influence our responses. One way to approach the question *"Why do we argue?"* would be to consider what sorts of things we don't argue about.

We don't argue about things we consider trivial
Hollihan and Baaske suggest that most of us tend not to argue about things we consider unimportant:

> Often we find ourselves in conversations where someone makes a statement that we disagree with, but our disagreement is so trivial that we need to decide whether the relational tension that might result from a public disagreement is warranted. Sometimes arguments are not worth the effort because the issue about which we differ is not very significant.

> (Hollihan & Baaske, 2005, p. 29)

We don't argue about ideas we can easily verify as true or false
Equally, it would be a waste of time to argue over ideas whose truth we can easily verify. For example, if you and a friend disagreed about the meaning of a word, you could just look it up in one or more dictionaries, since dictionaries codify the commonly understood meanings of words. Similarly, if you disagreed about when the moon rose last night, you could check the meteorological records for your area. And, if you disagreed about the number of street lamps on your street, you could go count them or accept the word of a credible source.

We don't argue about beliefs no one is prepared to give up
A third category of arguments we usually consider not worth having are those directed towards changing the beliefs, attitudes or behaviour of a firmly committed ideologue:

> Some people hold beliefs so strongly that they are not open to critical reflection. Many arguments over the merits of particular religious philosophies are of this type.... Such arguments would be especially difficult to accept if they came from someone outside the faith, since one might question both the arguer's knowledge of the religious teachings of [the faith in question] and his or her motives for seeking to discredit the faith.

> (Hollihan & Baaske, 2005, pp.29-30)

To summarise, we argue whenever we encounter situations characterised by **uncertainty**, where **proof** is unavailable and people can reasonably draw different conclusions from the available **evidence** (facts, artefacts and interpretation of facts). But, we do this only for issues we consider important enough to warrant the risk and effort associated with arguing.

We can now return to the question of distinguishing argument from explanation. In the example of your teacher asking you to explain why you were late for class, we assume (1) that your being late is not in dispute — both you and your teacher agree on this 'fact'; and, (2) that your teacher is asking for an explanation because she doesn't know why you were late and you ostensibly do. In other words, people seek explanations because they have a gap in their knowledge that they wish to bridge through information transfer. If your instructor accepts your explanation for your tardiness, then this brief communicative exchange will most likely end, the explanation having been sought and obtained.

What happens, however, if your teacher does *not* accept your explanation because she has her own suspicions about why you were late? Given your teacher's scepticism (doubts about your explanation), we now have the potential for a shift in genres from explanation to argument.

Argument researchers Edward Inch and Barbara Warnick (2010) emphasise that for any issue that you can think of, there is "*an imaginary line that separates what is accepted by the audience from what is not accepted*" (p.50, italics in original). Everything *below* this imaginary line represents what the audience accepts, and includes:

❖ commonplace beliefs and self-evident truths;

❖ empirical statements that the audience accepts as 'facts'; and,

❖ axioms and assumptions that the audience takes for granted.

The **level of dispute** is "the lowest common level that an audience is willing to accept" (Inch and Warnick, 2010, p.51). Everything below the imaginary (*level of dispute*) line represents **common ground** between arguer and audience; everything above it is open to dispute.

In an **established argument**, all three elements (claim, support and reasoning) lie below the level of dispute (see Figure 1.4, adapted from Inch & Warnick, 2010, p.52). So, there is nothing left to argue about. For example, the statement *The earth is spherical* is an accepted claim, an established 'fact' today because most contemporary audiences accept the evidence and reasoning supporting this claim.

Level of Dispute

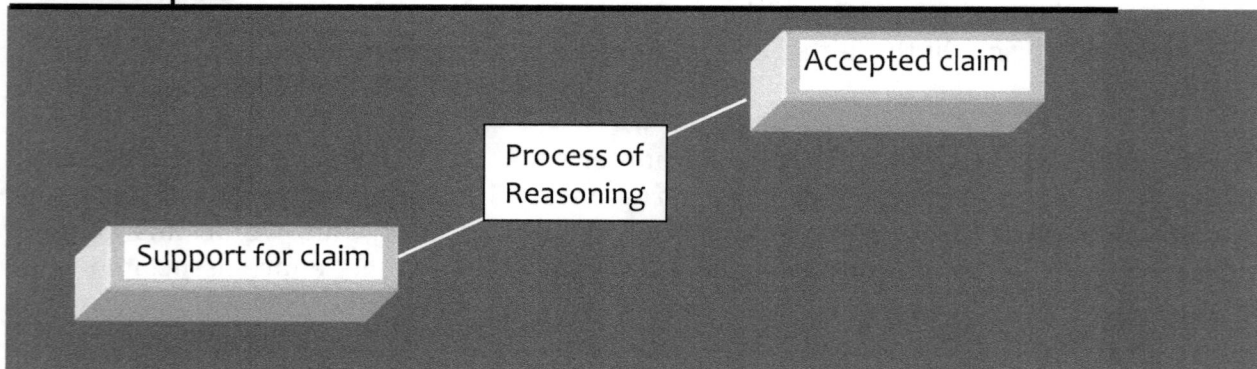

Figure 1.4　　**The level of dispute in an established argument**

In contrast, the same claim was an **arguable claim** in earlier times when people believed the earth was flat. The picture then would have looked as illustrated in Figure 1.5 (adapted from Inch & Warnick, 2010, p.51).

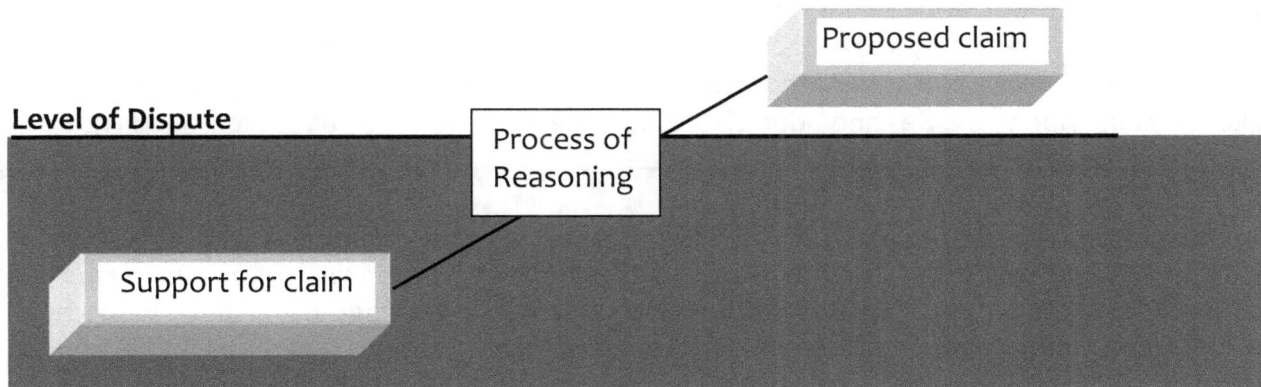

Figure 1.5   The level of dispute in an authentic argument

When designing an argument, the rhetor's first task is to discover where the level of dispute lies for the issue at hand so that s/he can build **common ground** with the audience, employing as evidence only those facts, artefacts and interpretations of fact that lie *below* the level of dispute for the particular audience being addressed. For example, it would be pointless to invoke God as support in an argument addressed to atheists, since this audience, by definition, does not accept His existence, let alone His edicts. For this audience, God lies *above* rather than *below* the level of dispute.

The **level of dispute** highlights the irony at the heart of argument. In order to argue productively, we must first establish what we agree on — the common ground that will serve as the shared foundation for resolving the disagreement between rhetor and audience. If we don't first ascertain what lies *below* the level of dispute, we cannot effectively address what lies *above* it (the claim that we wish our audience to accept).

Activity 1.4

Is this text (from Crider, 2005, pp.5-6) an argument or an explanation?

Eating is important. Because everyone eats, restaurants have an important social purpose. My favourite restaurant is McDonald's. I like McDonald's for three reasons.

First, I like McDonald's because the food is very good. The Big Mac is particularly tasty, so I order one every time I go there.

Second, I like McDonald's because the food is inexpensive. I can eat lunch for under four dollars. This means that I can eat there often.

Third, I like McDonald's because someone I don't like works there, and, while I enjoy my inexpensive lunch, I can watch him slave over the grill for minimum wage.

In conclusion, I like McDonald's because the food is good and inexpensive, and the staff entertaining.

> ## Comment on Activity 1.4
> For me, the text is an explanation because the author offers three reasons why s/he likes McDonald's without anticipating scepticism from her/his audience. Likes and dislikes are matters of personal taste, and it doesn't seem from the text that a choice needs to be made, between McDonald's and some other eatery. If I like the taste of garlic and you don't or you like watching horror movies and I don't, does it make sense to argue about it — why (not)?

In this section, we've considered the relationship between argument and explanation, surmising that although similar in structure, the two genres differ in terms of communicative purpose. **Explanations** seek to transfer knowledge from those who know to those who want to know in a context where the desire to know supersedes scepticism. In contrast, **arguments** seek to resolve disagreement about a truth claim, value claim or policy claim in a context of uncertainty, where **logical proof** is unavailable and a choice must be made between competing claims.

1.3   How are argument and persuasion related?

Some analysts use the terms *argument* and *persuasion*, interchangeably. Others (including myself) view argument as a subset of persuasion:

> Persuasion is concerned primarily with influencing the way people think or act, whereas argument is concerned with discovering and conveying our best judgments about the truth of things through an appeal to reason. All arguments involve persuasion, but [not] all persuasive acts...involve argument.
>
> (Ramage and Bean, 1995, p.3)

The online *Encyclopaedia Britannica* describes persuasion as *the process by which a person's attitudes or behaviour, are without duress, influenced by communications from other people*. This notion of persuasion as a non-coercive communicative process is a timely reminder that we can be influenced by means other than persuasion, ranging from torture, brainwashing, drugs and hormones to incentives and disincentives of various kinds, including bribes and fines. The adage *the pen is mightier than the sword* polarises these means of influence with the sword representing violent action at one end of the spectrum and the pen representing rhetorical or symbolic action (see speech act theory's *saying is doing* assumption in section 3.8).

Both argument and persuasion represent non-coercive communication aimed at influencing beliefs, attitudes and behaviour. The difference is that persuaders seek to obtain assent, whereas arguers hope to gain *critical assent* (see section 4.10) Persuaders need only ask *How can I get you to change your mind?* Arguers, however, must consider a second, equally important question *When should I assent to your views, thus changing my mind?* (see Figure 1.6) because rationality demands that we revise our stance, when there are compelling reasons to do so.

	EXPLANATION	PERSUASION	ARGUMENT
Structure	*X because Y*	*X because Y*	*X because Y*
Context	knowledge gap	uncertainty and doubt	uncertainty and doubt
Purpose	to transfer knowledge from those who know to those who want to know	to obtain assent: *How do I get you to change your mind?*	to obtain critical assent: *How do I get you to change your mind? And, when should I assent to your views?*

Figure 1.6   Argument, explanation and persuasion distinguished

Here's how mathematician George Polya explains the demands of rationality:

> In our own personal life we often cling to illusions. That is, we do not dare to examine certain beliefs which could be easily contradicted by experience because we are afraid of upsetting our emotional balance. There may be circumstances in which it is not unwise to cling to illusions, but in science we need a very different attitude... This attitude...requires saying "maybe" and "perhaps" in a thousand different shades. It requires many other things, especially the following three:
> First, we should be ready to revise any one of our beliefs.
> Second, we should change a belief when there is compelling reason to change it.
> Third, we should not change a belief wantonly, without some good reason.
>
> (Polya, 1954, pp. 7-8)

Needless to say, argument is integral to knowledge construction, the process of discovering and testing the grounds for rational belief. Sceptical audiences demand strong reasons for accepting a claim because they know that human knowledge is fallible and subject to revision, as new evidence comes in.

Most people think of scientific knowledge as the gold standard of human knowledge. But, even science does not provide absolute certainty, only certainty *beyond reasonable doubt*, as physicist Richard Feynman eloquently explains:

> The scientist has a lot of experience with ignorance and doubt and uncertainty, and this experience is of very great importance, I think. When a scientist doesn't know the answer to a problem, he is ignorant. When he has a hunch as to what the result is, he is uncertain. And when he is pretty darn sure of what the result is going to be, he is still in some doubt. We have found it of paramount importance that in order to progress we must recognize our ignorance and leave room for doubt. Scientific knowledge is a body of statements of varying degrees of certainty—some most unsure, some nearly sure, but none absolutely certain.

(Feynman, 1999, p.146)

What this means is that arguers must anticipate and be prepared to respond to objections and alternative viewpoints to their own. If they cannot respond satisfactorily to counter-arguments, rationality demands that they modify their position accordingly, since it would be irrational to hold firm to a position supported by weak or equivocal reasons.

1.4   Inquiry vs. advocacy arguments

In section 1.1, we saw that claims can be classified into truth claims, value claims and policy claims. These three types of claims serve as the basis for a taxonomy in which arguments are classified according to the type of claim being argued (see sections 4.4 to 4.7). Argument theorists George Ziegelmueller and Jack Kay (1997), meanwhile, distinguish two broad classes of argument, inquiry arguments and advocacy arguments, based on the communicative purpose of the argument.

Inquiry arguments are so-named because they're motivated by a desire to understand ourselves and the world around us, as we inquire into questions of:

❖   truth (*What is X? How does X work? What are the causes and effects of X?*);

❖   value (*Is X 'good' or 'bad', morally, legally, aesthetically...?*); and,

❖   policy (*Should we or shouldn't we do X?*)

Not surprisingly, inquiry arguments play a central role in knowledge construction, and are used primarily (but not exclusively) by academics. Others who engage in inquiry arguments include detectives trying to identify the murderer in a homicide case, public health officials trying to identify the source of pollution in a village, and business groups trying to learn what kinds of advertising are effective in a particular country or culture. Arguments which ask *Does mobile phone usage lead to brain tumours? Do oldest children make good bosses?* and *What should we do with the terminally ill?* are all examples of inquiry arguments.

Whereas inquiry arguments are curiosity-driven, **advocacy arguments** are made by those advocating a belief, attitude or behaviour to which they've already committed. Advocacy arguments predominate in the civic, legal and political arenas, as advocates ranging from politicians to non-profit organisations lobby diverse audiences, promoting their respective agendas. Someone arguing that *we should spend less on exploring space and more on alleviating poverty* would be advocating a change in behaviour in terms of how our tax dollars are spent. Someone arguing that *the homeless don't deserve our contempt* is proposing a change in attitude towards the homeless. And, someone arguing that *capital punishment does not deter crime* is advocating a change in belief about the efficacy of capital punishment as a deterrent to crime.

Activity 1.5

What kind of argument — inquiry or advocacy — might each of these utterances launch? Explain clearly and concisely how you arrived at your answers.

(1) *The Second World War was a just war.*

(2) *What were the real reasons for the second Gulf war?*

Whether we're dealing with inquiry or advocacy arguments, it's important not to fall into the trap of viewing all argument as an adversarial zero-sum game in which the winner takes all. Granted, this is the model used in trials and academic debate competitions. But, this model of argument in which two parties lock horns in verbal combat to persuade an impartial third-party of the merits of their case is *not* a logical entailment of either inquiry or advocacy arguments. You'll learn in section 3.2 that arguments can be **dyadic exchanges** (where arguers address each other) or **triadic exchanges** (where arguers address a third party). **Politeness theory** (see section 3.7) in turn suggests that adopting an adversarial stance in a dyadic argument is more likely to hinder than to help. After all, how willing would you be to engage cooperatively with someone treating you as the enemy?

1.5   Descriptive vs. prescriptive approaches

When investigating a phenomenon, it's hard to devote equal attention to all aspects of it. So, we necessarily foreground some aspects, allowing other aspects to recede into the background. This means that different people studying the same phenomenon can produce different analyses, based on their different priorities and perspectives.

Some investigators adopt a prescriptive approach while others prefer a descriptive approach. Researchers adopting a **descriptive approach** analyse the object of their inquiry in order to understand how something works. In contrast, researchers adopting a normative, or **prescriptive approach** tend to evaluate the phenomenon being investigated, since their goal is to articulate how things *ought to be* rather than how they *are*.

Given the (legitimate) goal of helping students argue better, most argument textbooks adopt a normative approach, inviting students to evaluate arguments so as to emulate the good and avoid the bad. This volume takes a descriptive approach in that it is not a *how to* manual but a *how does it work* study.

Our goal is not to evaluate the success or failure of a persuasion message but to understand how arguers adaptively employ the resources of language at the level of lexico-grammar, coherence relations and rhetorical structure to invent, organise and style their arguments in response to different audiences and issues.

1.6　Three complementary perspectives on argument

According to Joseph Wenzel (1990), argument researchers tend to adopt one of three complementary perspectives (logical, dialectical or rhetorical), approaching their object of inquiry. Wenzel likens this to looking at a building from the front, the side, and the top, emphasising that these are NOT three kinds of argument, but three ways of looking at argument. For example, if you look at the left-most and middle items in Figure 1.7, you might think you were looking at a circle and a rectangle respectively, not realizing that all three images represent three complementary views of a cylinder seen from the top, the side and in three dimensions.

Figure 1.7　　Three views of a cylinder

Each perspective views argument from a different vantage point, prioritising different aspects, as summarised in Figure 1.8.

Perspective	LOGICAL	DIALECTICAL	RHETORICAL
Argument viewed as	product of logic	procedure for critical decision-making	process of persuasion
Focus is on	claim, premises and reasoning	presentation of all relevant views	invention, organisation, and style of argument
A 'good' argument is	sound	orderly and fair	convincing

Figure 1.8　　Three complementary perspectives on argument

The **logical perspective** views argument as a product of logic. Within this perspective, analysing an argument involves stripping it down to its component parts (claim, premises and reasoning) in order to judge whether the argument is **sound.** A sound argument is one in which all the premises are true and the reasoning is valid, thereby leading to a true conclusion.

One disadvantage of the logical perspective, however, is its failure to acknowledge that arguments are context-dependent and audience-bound. The British philosopher Stephen Toulmin attempted to address the shortcomings of formal logic by creating a model of argument analysis still used by many argument teachers and researchers today. Unfortunately, Toulmin's (1958) model still treats argument primarily as a logical construction composed of claim, data, warrants, and backing, rather than as a communicative exchange.

The **dialectical perspective** in turn views argument as a procedure for making critical decisions. This perspective acknowledges that good decisions require clear thinking promoted by orderly procedures characterised by integrity and fairness. Accordingly, it focuses on the standards of behaviour which promote critical decision-making in formal settings like parliament and law courts as well as informal settings like family negotiations. Within the dialectical perspective, an argument needs to measure up to four C's to be considered orderly and fair. The arguers must:

❖ *cooperate* by following procedures;

❖ address the topic as *comprehensively* as possible;

❖ be *candid* in opening ideas up for close scrutiny; and,

❖ be *critical* in reaching a decision based on rigorous testing of alternative positions.

A contemporary version of the dialectical perspective is Frans van Eemeren and Rob Grootendorst's (2004) pragma-dialectical theory, which treats argument as a complex of speech acts for resolving conflict: "After describing the stages through which a rational discussion must pass to achieve resolution, they [Eemeren and Grootendorst] consider the various kinds of speech acts that are dialectically relevant to each discussion stage" (Wenzel, 1990, p.22).

The approach taken in this volume resonates most with the **rhetorical perspective**, given my attempt to synthesise contemporary linguistics and Aristotelian rhetoric. The rhetorical perspective views argument as a communicative process in which two or more arguers seek to influence their own and/or others' beliefs, attitudes or behaviours, in different settings. And, within this perspective, a *good* argument is a **convincing** argument. As rhetoricians Chaim Perelman and Lucie Olbrechts-Tyteca (1969) explain, the difference between *persuasion* and *conviction* is that arguers may succeed at convincing without persuading the audience to act because persuasion is determined not by the arguer but by the audience.

There is no way, in other words, of guaranteeing that an audience *will* be persuaded by a message. If that *were* possible, we would have a recipe or formula capable of persuading all sorts of people (including ourselves) to think (believe), feel (value) and act (behave) as we want them to, in all sorts of situations. What rhetorical analysts seek to understand is how specific rhetorical strategies may affect particular audiences, in particular times and places, which is also our goal in this volume. In the next chapter, we take a closer look at rhetorical analysis, tracing its origins all the way back to the birth of Greek democracy in the fifth century BC.

References

Belcher, Diane. (1997). An Argument for non-adversarial argumentation: On the relevance of the feminist critique of academic discourse to L2 writing pedagogy. *Journal of Second Language Writing 6*(1), pp.1-21.

Chapman, Graham, Idle, Eric, Gilliam Terry, and Jones, Terry. (1999). *Monty Python's Flying Circus Vol. 2*. London: Methuen.

Creme, Phyllis & Lea, Mary R. (2008). *Writing at university: A guide for students* (3rd edition). Open University Press (McGraw Hill).

Crider, Scott F. (2005). *The Office of Assertion: An art of rhetoric for the academic essay.* Wilmington, Delaware: ISI Books.

Encyclopaedia Britannica. Retrieved on June 8, 2011 from http://www.britannica.com/EBchecked/topic/453093/persuasion

Feynman, Richard. (1955/1999). The Value of Science. In Robbins, J. (Ed.) *The pleasure of finding things out: the best short works of Richard P. Feynman.* Cambridge, MA: Perseus, pp. 141-150.

Gottman, John Mordecai. (1994). *What Predicts Divorce?* Hillsdale, NJ: Lawrence Erlbaum Associates.

Hollihan, Thomas A. and Baaske, Kevin T. (2005). *Arguments and Arguing* (2nd edition) Long Grove, Illinois: Waveland Press.

Inch, Edward S. and Warnick, Barbara. (2010). *Critical Thinking and Communication: The Use of Reason in Argument* (6th edition). Boston: Allyn & Bacon.

Jackson, Sally & Jacobs, Scott. (1980). Structure of Conversational Argument: Pragmatic Bases for the Enythmeme. *Quarterly Journal of Speech* 66(3), 251-265.

Lakoff, George and Johnson, Mark. (1981). *Metaphors we Live By.* Chicago: The University of Chicago Press.

O'Keefe, Daniel. (1977). Two Concepts of Argument. *The Journal of the American Forensic Association* Vol. XIII, No. 3, 121-128.

Perelman, Chaim & Olbrechts-Tyteca, Lucie. (1969). *The New Rhetoric: A Treatise on Argumentation.* Trans. J Wilkinson & P. Weaver. Notre Dame: University of Notre Dame Press.

Polya, George. (1954). *Mathematics and Plausible Reasoning, Volume I: Induction and Analogy in Mathematics.* Princeton University Press.

Ramage, John D. and Bean, John C. (1995). *Writing Arguments*: *A rhetoric with readings* (3rd edition) Boston: Allyn & Bacon.

Tannen, Deborah. (1998). *The Argument Culture: Moving from debate to dialogue.* New York: Random House.

Tannen, Deborah. (2002). Agonism in academic discourse. *Journal of Pragmatics 34*, 1651-1669.

Toulmin, Stephen. (1958). *The Uses of Argument.* Cambridge University Press.

van Eemeren, Frans H. and Grootendorst, Rob. (2004). *A systematic theory of argumentation: the pragma-dialectical approach.* Cambridge University Press.

Wenzel, Joseph. (1990). Three Perspectives on Argument: Rhetoric, Dialectic, Logic. In R. Trapp & J. Schuetz (Eds.) *Perspectives on Argumentation: Essays in Honor of Wayne Brockriede.* Illinois: Waveland Press, pp. 9-26.

Ziegelmueller, George W. and Kay, Jack. (1997). *Argumentation: inquiry and advocacy* (3rd edition). Boston: Allyn and Bacon.

Chapter 2 Rhetoric

What's the difference between rhetoric and rhetrickery?

What are Aristotle's three genres of rhetoric?

How can Goodnight's (1982) argument spheres help in rhetorical analysis?

How can Hymes's (1972) SPEAKING mnemonic help in rhetorical analysis?

2.1   What does rhetoric encompass?

We ended the previous chapter with a brief look at three complementary perspectives on argument — logical, dialectical and rhetorical. All three perspectives emerged in ancient Greece around the fifth century BC, concomitant with the emergence of Greek democracy. The timeline makes sense when we recall the civic ideal of classical Greek democracy — free people communicating freely to serve the common good of the city-state. As argument researcher Joseph Wenzel (1990) remarks, "upon that ideal rests the interests that motivate rhetoric, dialectic and logic: the interest in adapting speech to audiences and situations; the interest in cooperative methods for decision-making; and the interest in devising standards of rational judgment" (p.12).

As mentioned in the previous chapter, my approach resonates most with the rhetorical perspective, which views argument as an emergent phenomenon. As rhetorician Wayne Brockriede emphasises (1975/1990), "Human activity does not usefully constitute an argument until some person perceives what is happening as an argument" (p.4). Discourse analysts Sally Jacobs and Scott Jackson (1982) observe that wherever there is a potential for people to engage in conversation, there is a potential for them to disagree and thus to argue. Jacobs and Jackson's research focuses on conversational arguments — how arguments begin, how they're implied and recognised by conversational partners, and how their development affects the organisation of broader conversational episodes. Jacobs and Jackson's (1982) goal in examining informal conversational arguments is to discover features of argument that may be absent or downplayed in public oratory.

2.2   Rhetoric and rhetrickery

Despite the continued interest in rhetoric, the term itself has always been much-maligned and misunderstood, often used pejoratively, as in *empty rhetoric* or *mere rhetoric*, to refer to manipulative communication — a process of verbal trickery, or *rhetrickery* (Booth, 2005, p.379) by means of which rhetors gain an unfair advantage over their audience without much regard for truth or ethics. Certainly, that was how the Greek philosopher Plato viewed rhetoric as taught by the Greek sophists of his day. His student, Aristotle, however, saw the importance of rhetoric in situations where three factors converge:

1. **We have to decide between two competing choices;**

2. **each choice has some merit to it; and,**

3. **logical proof is unavailable.**

Aristotle defined rhetoric as "the faculty of discovering the possible means of persuasion in reference to any subject whatever" (I.2.I cited in Crider, 2005, p.5) adding that "what makes one a sophist is not the faculty but the moral purpose" (I.1.14. cited in Crider 2005, p.4). As educator Scott Crider (2005) neatly summarises, "rhetoric is persuasion aimed at the truth; sophistry is persuasion aimed only at the appearance of truth" (p.4). In other words, once rhetoric loses its ethical moorings, it devolves into rhetrickery.

The second thing to bear in mind is that rhetoric is *not* a formula, even though this is the stock in trade of many rhetoric textbooks. Here's one example that Crider (2005) highlights — the Five-Paragraph Essay formula taught to most high school students:

> The "rule" is this: every essay has five paragraphs — an introduction, three points, and a conclusion. Three other formulae follow: The introduction should begin generally and funnel into one's thesis, the last sentence of the first paragraph; the next three paragraphs should be numbered — first, second, and third; and, finally, the conclusion should summarize the essay and funnel out towards some very general point.
>
> (Crider, 2005, p.3)

Rules of thumb such as these are energy-saving devices that encapsulate human knowledge pithily. But, they can also short-circuit the process of critical and creative discovery, if followed mechanically and mindlessly.

2.3   Rhetoric as a critical observational faculty

Rhetoric, as Aristotle defined it, is a faculty of the human mind directed towards finding the permissible and (best) possible means of persuasion for a given issue and audience. Rhetoric thus encompasses not just a means of producing (ethical) persuasion but also of interpreting it. As rhetorician Jack Selzer (2004) explains, rhetorical analysis is a process of close critical reading:

> Aristotle's definition actually calls rhetoric a 'faculty' (*dunamis*) of "observing" (*theorein*) the available (sometimes glossed as possible or permissible) means of persuasion in any given case...rhetoric is a trained faculty or capacity for analytically observing what is both possible to say in a given situation (an inventory of all possible arguments) and what is allowable (what lines of argument ought to be persuasive; what one can get away with; what one should assent to or not; etc.)
>
> (Walker, personal communication, cited in Selzer, 2004, p.280)

Our focus in this volume is on rhetoric as a critical observational faculty, and rhetorical analysis as a process of discovering how a persuasion message seeks to achieve its communicative purpose. Our objective is to become more finely attuned to the ways in which rhetors adapt their language use at the level of lexico-grammar, coherence relations and rhetorical structure as they seek to persuade audiences, eloquently and ethically. As Selzer (2004) puts it, "[r]hetorical analysis is an effort to read interpretively, with an eye toward understanding a message fully and how that message is crafted to earn a particular response" (p.282).

At this point, you may be wondering whether all communication isn't ultimately aimed at persuasion. Rhetorician Kenneth Burke (1950) asserts that rhetoric is *"rooted in an essential function of language itself,...the use of language as a symbolic means of inducing cooperation in beings that by nature respond to symbols"* (p.43, italics in original). Taken to its endpoint, such a view would suggest that the entire field of semiotics (the study of humanity's propensity for symbol use in all areas of life) could in fact be co-opted into the domain of rhetoric. Selzer and Crowley's (1999) book *Rhetorical Bodies* attempts to make just this case — that hair styles, clothing, musculature, prosthetics and piercings embody arguments about particular versions of beauty. Our primary focus, however, is on persuasion achieved through language rather than through other symbolic systems such as architecture, dance or painting.

2.4   Textual and contextual analysis

As Selzer (2004) emphasises, there are "many approaches to rhetorical analysis, and no one 'correct' way to do it: there is no simple recipe for it" (p.283). Selzer himself helpfully places these different approaches along a continuum ranging from textual analysis, at one end, to contextual analysis, at the other. ***Textual analysis*** emphasises text over context, offering a close reading of the text's design, whereas ***contextual analysis*** emphasises context over text:

> attempt[-ing] to reconstruct a rhetorical moment within which a particular rhetorical event (the one under scrutiny) took place, to create a thick description of the (sometimes complex) cultural environment that existed when that rhetorical event took place, and then to depend on that recreation to produce clues about the persuasive tactics and appeals that are visible in the performance in question.
>
> (Selzer, 2004, p.283)

The good news is that we don't have to choose between the two, since our aim is to understand how persuasion works by paying close attention to the interplay between text, context and subtext.

2.5   Text, context and subtext

All discourse occurs in specific linguistic and situational contexts. **Linguistic context** refers to surrounding text, what has been said and done by those present, while **situational context** refers to the socio-historical setting of a communicative exchange. To interpret meaning accurately, we need to interpret all texts within their linguistic and situational contexts.

Activity 2.1

How would you respond to the question *How are you?* asked by

(1) a friend you meet along a corridor? (2) a doctor in her office?

Comment on Activity 2.1

Although the question takes the same form, I would interpret its function differently, based on contextual clues like who's doing the asking, when and where. My answer to my friend might take the form *I'm well. Thanks. How are you?* I wouldn't, however, offer this response to the doctor, for two reasons. One, in my mental model of doctor-patient interactions, doctors ask questions in order to diagnose a patient's illness. Two, I don't go to the doctor's unless I'm unwell. So, the response *I'm well. Thanks* would probably seem odd, unless I were at the doctor's office for a routine check-up.

In short, I'd interpret my friend's *How are you?* as a greeting, an instance of what linguists call *phatic communion* (language used to grease the wheels of social interaction). In contrast, I'd interpret the doctor's *How are you?* as a polite means (compared to the ruder alternatives: *What's the matter with you? What's wrong with you?*) of eliciting the medical complaint that has brought me to the doctor's office.

Context provides a frame for accurately interpreting text. As the context changes, so does our understanding of what the text is saying because meaning is functional, emerging from the context of use rather than resting solely in the words used.

Secondly, all communication involves a certain amount of mind-reading because people don't always say what they mean or mean what they say. When you see an iceberg, you know that you're seeing just the tip of the iceberg and that a large part remains submerged. Similarly, discourse comprises **text** (what a speaker says) and **subtext** (what a speaker means or implies). You may be wondering *Why not just make everything explicit?* The short answer is that comprehensively explicit messages would be insufferably long, intolerably tedious, and entirely confusing.

Like most human pursuits, communication adheres to the **Law of Least Effort**, or the **Law of Maximal Economy**. In order to make new information salient, 'old news' (what discourse analysts call **given information**) is condensed or omitted altogether to make room for **new information**. Consider the following exchange:

Husband: *Have you seen my glasses?*
Wife: *No.*

The wife omits the clause *I haven't seen your glasses* from her answer because it is *given information,* information that has been activated in both participants' minds by the husband's initial utterance. We condense or omit *given information* because we assume that our addressees can recover this information from context.

A second reason we don't always communicate explicitly has to do with politeness (see section 3.7). Suppose your friend asks *Did I get the answer to that puzzle wrong?* You could answer *Yes.* But, you could also imply a *Yes* by saying *Well, you didn't get it right,* allowing your friend to infer that he got the answer wrong, based on his linguistic knowledge that *right* and *wrong* are complementary (mutually exclusive) antonyms. Figure 2.1 crystallises the relationship between **text, subtext** and **context**. To bridge the gap between what speakers say and what they mean, addressees interpret text in context.

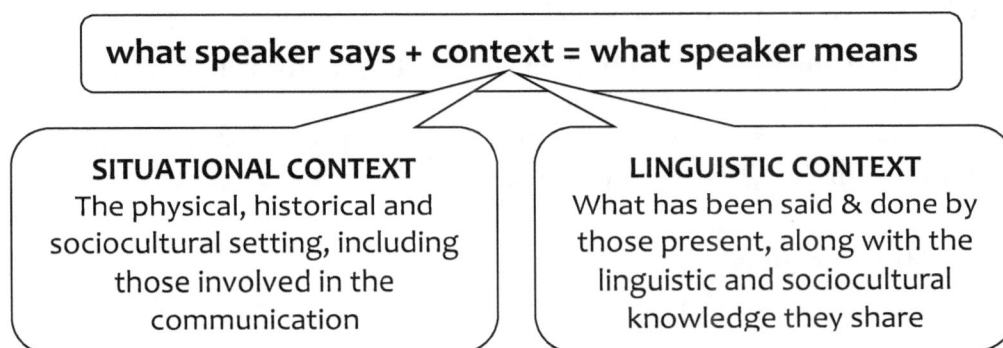

what speaker says + context = what speaker means

SITUATIONAL CONTEXT
The physical, historical and sociocultural setting, including those involved in the communication

LINGUISTIC CONTEXT
What has been said & done by those present, along with the linguistic and sociocultural knowledge they share

Figure 2.1   **Context as an interpretive frame for text**

2.6   HOW you say WHAT you say

The distinction between explicit and implicit communication highlights the two sides of the communication coin: WHAT speakers say (substance) and HOW they say it (style). As we shall see in chapter 6, style is not an ornamental extra or decorative detail that we add after we've planned our messages. Rather, style and substance are inextricably linked. To change the style is to change the substance. And, just as we expect consistency between words and actions (crystallised in the adage *Walk the talk*), so also there is an expectation that style and substance will work together to create a credible message.

Activity 2.2

Say *Please stop crying* in as many different ways as you can think of. If you're with friends, listen carefully to HOW each of your friends utters these words, then find an appropriate **performative verb** such as *instructed, commanded, cajoled, teased, comforted* or *barked at* to report the speech act performed in each version.

Activity 2.3

Language is a design tool for communicating various kinds of messages. As all designers know, there is no strict one-to-one correspondence between form and function. One form can have multiple functions, and *vice versa*. If you wanted someone to stop crying, you could say *Please stop crying*. But, you could also word your message in other ways. Think of as many possibilities as you can, then categorise each utterance, stating clearly and concisely the basis you used for your classification system.

For a more detailed discussion of the stylistic resources used by rhetors to enact and amplify the significance of their persuasion messages, see chapter 6.

2.7 Aristotle's three genres of rhetoric

According to argument researcher Joseph Wenzel (1990), rhetorical occasions emerge whenever "people find themselves in situations where it seems that persuading others will serve some purpose — to solve a problem, bring about a happier state of affairs, or just enhance their relationships" (p.18). Faced with a persuasion message, we can ask four questions:

- ❖ **What occasioned the discourse?**
- ❖ **What is its purpose?**
- ❖ **What issue is being addressed?**
- ❖ **Who are the addresser and addressee(s)?**

These questions highlight the contingent or adaptive nature of discourse — that we do not talk or write in the same way to all people at all times, but customise our messages, fitting our words to the situation, audience and purpose at hand.

In ancient Greece, there were three main forums for public persuasion — the law, politics and civic ceremonies. Based on the audience addressed and the activities conducted in these forums, Aristotle identified three genres of rhetoric (see Figure 2.2 and section 4.2).

- ❖ **Forensic rhetoric** was practised in the courtroom, and focused on determining the truth concerning past action.
- ❖ **Deliberative rhetoric** occurred in citizens' assemblies, and deliberated the benefit or harmfulness of a future course of action.
- ❖ **Epideictic rhetoric** was displayed at ceremonial occasions and reinforced or reframed communal identity by praising heroes and condemning common enemies.

Genre	FORENSIC	DELIBERATIVE	EPIDEICTIC
Issue	truth	policy	value
Purpose	to affirm or deny past action	to exhort or dissuade from future action	to praise or blame present action
Setting	courtroom	citizens' assembly	civic ceremony
Audience	jurors	voters	spectators
Examples	prosecution and defence speeches	sermon, policy speech, didactic poem	inaugural and farewell addresses

Figure 2.2   Aristotle's three genres of rhetoric

2.8   Personal, technical and public argument spheres

Aristotle focused on public persuasion, but contemporary rhetoricians are equally interested in private persuasion. Thomas Goodnight (1982) suggests that arguments can be placed in three overlapping *spheres* — personal, technical or public. Goodnight (1982) depicts these spheres as overlapping because an argument that starts in one sphere can shift to the other two spheres, and be conducted in all three spheres, concurrently or consecutively.

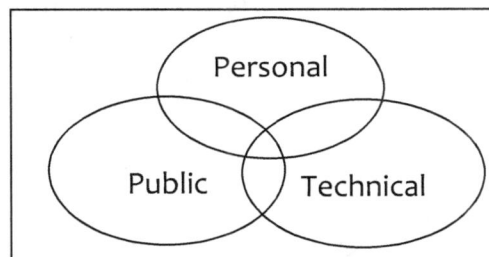

Figure 2.3   Personal, technical and public argument spheres

The **personal argument sphere** contains arguments between close friends and family, conducted in private with fluid rules of persuasion, i.e. the rules of argument and the standards for evaluating arguments tend to be interpersonal or relational, best understood by the participants themselves, based on the nature of their relationship. The next time you argue with your boyfriend or girlfriend, parents or siblings, best friend or spouse, see if you can discover the different rules that apply or that you make up as you go along, when arguing with these different individuals.

The **technical argument sphere** contains arguments between fellow specialists, conducted in relatively formal settings with formal rules of argument. Although not set in stone, the rules of argument in this sphere tend to evolve fairly slowly because they have to be accepted by all members of the relevant community of practice. And, in order to be accepted by the expert members of the community, novice members have to learn the rules encompassing what can be argued and how it should be argued within their specialist domain, i.e. what counts as an arguable claim and how that claim can and should be supported in terms of legitimate reasoning and evidence (*facts, artefacts* and *interpretation of facts*).

Consider, for example, how lawyers argue a case in court. There are definite procedures that must be followed in terms of who (defence or prosecution) can speak, to whom (the judge, jury or witnesses), and for what purpose (eliciting testimony, cross-examining a witness, raising an objection, redirecting a witness statement).

Similarly, what counts as evidence is strictly defined — hearsay, for example, is usually inadmissible, except where the law allows for hearsay exceptions. An integral part of the training that law students receive in law school entails enculturation into the rhetoric of the law, i.e. what it means to argue like a lawyer. The same process of enculturation applies to novices in other subject domains, who must similarly acquire the rules of argument of their chosen specialisation.

The **public argument sphere** contains arguments made in public, addressing issues of interest and concern to the public. Examples include speeches made by politicians to their constituents as well as editorials, letters to the editor, opinion pieces and commentaries disseminated via print, broadcast and online media for public perusal. Arguments in the public sphere form the bedrock of democratic government, allowing ordinary citizens to address a mass audience. As David Zarefsky (1998, cited in Inch and Warnick, 2010) observes, public sphere argument "represents the ideal of full and equal participation and deliberation by those with interests in a decision" (p.18).

2.9   Hymes's SPEAKING heuristic for discourse analysis

The main objective of this book is to help you develop a portable rhetorical toolkit for analysing argument design. Anthropologist Dell Hymes (1972) created the **SPEAKING** mnemonic (see Figure 2.4) as an aid for close textual analysis.

We will be scrutinizing the eight elements highlighted by Hymes in the chapters to come. For now, we look briefly at the letters S, N and G, representing Situation, Norms and Genres, respectively. Since discourse is situated language use, the first step in analysing any discourse is to situate the text in its linguistic and situational context.

Hymes (1972) divides **situation** into the physical and socio-historical *setting* (time and place) and the *scene* (cultural event or activity) being enacted. **Setting** answers the question *When and where are we?* while *scene* answers the question *What are we doing?* It's important to consider both physical and socio-historical setting because language evolves across time and varies across space. For example, the word *gay* did not always mean 'homosexual', while the utterance *My cousin is a homely girl* means different things in

British and American varieties of English. As we saw in Activity 2.1, paying attention to context is crucial to accurate interpretation and analysis.

S	*Setting* *Scene*	Physical and socio-historical time and place Cultural event or activity engaged in
P	*Participants*	Addresser and Audience
E	*Ends*	Purpose and Outcome
A	*Acts*	Form and Function of message
K	*Key*	Tone (Addresser's attitude to issue & audience)
I	*Instrumentalities*	Medium, Mode and Channel of communication
N	*Norms*	Expectations governing behaviour
G	*Genres*	Text-types

Figure 2.4   Hymes's (1972) SPEAKING mnemonic

Whereas *setting* identifies the physical and socio-historical time and place of a communicative exchange, *scene* identifies the cultural event or activity taking place, whether this is a soccer game, a cocktail party or a graduation ceremony. *Scene* takes into account that discourse is a form of social action and that all language users display both grammatical and communicative competence. Grammatical competence encompasses language users' knowledge of the sounds and words of their language and how to combine these to form grammatical sentences, whereas communicative competence refers to language users' ability to deploy grammatical competence appropriately in different contexts.

In some activities, language serves a peripheral rather than a central role (see Activity 1.1). For example, if you go to the movies with a group of friends, they won't expect you to maintain a conversation during the movie. Similarly, a soccer game requires minimal use of language unlike a soccer commentary, which could not exist without language. For activities like meetings and lectures, similarly, language is not an optional extra but a necessity.

When analysing *scene*, it's important to remember that some events may be unique to a culture or at least more common in some cultures than others — a cocktail party, for instance, would be anathema in cultures proscribing alcohol. Secondly, even if a social event is common across several cultures, there may be subtle nuances that distinguish them. For example, in exploring the discourse of academic research, genre analyst John Swales (2004) found several cultural differences in the way that the PhD defence, oral examination, *viva* or *disputas* is conducted in the US, the UK and continental Europe, respectively. Equally, hatchings, matchings, and dispatchings, more politely known as births, weddings and funerals are common to all societies, but exhibit cultural variation in terms of how they are rhetorically performed, i.e. who gets to speak to whom, when, how, and for what purpose. In western wedding receptions, for instance, it is customary for the bridegroom and the father of the bride to give speeches, with the best man assuming the role of master of ceremonies, inviting and thanking speakers for their contributions. This may not be the norm in other cultures.

2.10 Communication norms

The notion of customary behaviour leads us to Hymes's (1972) communication **norms**, community expectations comprising unspoken rules about what's normal (typical) and abnormal (atypical) behaviour for a given communicative activity. Often, we discover a norm only when we violate it, drawing comment on our aberrant behaviour. Since different norms hold for different activities and cultures, communicative competence involves acquiring multiple mental models, schemas or scripts about what is appropriate and inappropriate behaviour in particular *settings* and *scenes*. For example, family dinners can be achieved without language. But, whether or not a silent family dinner is atypical (anomalous, odd or deviant) depends on community norms.

Norms set the standard for what a community considers acceptable and unacceptable, which linguists label unmarked and marked choices, respectively. **Unmarked choices** are the **default options** that discourse participants consider unremarkable because they fit community norms. In contrast, **marked choices** represent **deviations from one or more norms**. Norms govern all aspects of discourse, influencing what can be said, how it can be said, to whom, when, where and why (for what purpose). In the next chapter, we consider some of the norms governing polite behaviour, drawing on insights from speech act theory and politeness theory. For now, we end our preview of Hymes's SPEAKING heuristic with a brief look at the notion of genre.

2.11 What is a genre?

Like the terms *rhetoric* and *argument*, *genre* is defined somewhat differently in different disciplines, focusing either on form or function. Definitions of the three main literary genres (poetry, prose and drama), for instance, focus on textual form, as do definitions of story types in folk studies.

Rhetorician Carolyn Miller (1984), however, argues that "a rhetorically sound definition of genre must be centered not on the substance or form of discourse but on the action it is used to accomplish" (p.151). Reinforcing this idea, genre analyst John Swales (1990) defines a genre as "a class of communicative events, the members of which share some set of communicative purposes" which shapes the genre's form by constraining content and stylistic choices (p.58). In accord with the assumption that form follows function, Swales advises genre analysts to prioritise communicative purpose as the key criterion for identifying and distinguishing genres.

Swales's recommendation makes sense if we consider that genres emerge as a response to recurrent communicative needs. As linguist James Martin (1985) observes, "Genres are how things get done, when language is used to accomplish them" (p.250). Or, as rhetorician Charles Bazerman explains it:

> Genres are not just forms. Genres are forms of life, ways of being. They are frames for social action. They are environments for learning. They are locations within which meaning is constructed. Genres shape the thoughts we form and the communications by which we interact. Genres are the familiar places we go to create intelligible communicative action with each other and the guideposts we use to explore the familiar.
>
> (Bazerman, 1997, p.19)

Genres, or text-types, obey the Law of Least Effort in that they represent our attempt **not** to reinvent the wheel. A genre emerges in response to a recurring need. If a genre meets the need, more and more people will use it, thereby establishing that genre as the preferred *solution* for the communicative *problem* in question. The labels we assign genres often describe the genre's form and/or function. The 'bad news letter', for example is a genre we employ to communicate bad news in the form of a letter. The communicative purpose (relaying bad news) guides *what* we say (selection of content), *when* we say it (sequencing of content) and *how* we say it (styling of content).

Like languages and cultures, genres evolve over time and vary across space. As Swales (1990) explains, a set of genres is an open class, with new members emerging and old ones decaying as communicative needs change. Genres thus represent typified textual configurations that are *stabilized-for-now* (Schryer, 1993), which evolve alongside communicative needs, resulting in new and possibly hybrid genres. Some genres evolve slowly. The research article, for example, has not changed much in 400 years, as Charles Bazerman's (1988) book-length study of the experimental science article illustrates. In contrast, computer-mediated genres tend to evolve far more quickly, as evidenced by newly emergent genres like SMS and tweet recipes, resulting from technological advances in mobile telephony and online social media.

Needless to say, it can sometimes be hard to tell whether or not two texts belong to the same genre because membership within a genre is not an all-or-nothing phenomenon. As Swales (1990) makes clear, exemplars of genres vary in their prototypicality because the boundaries separating one genre from another have fuzzy edges. The philosopher Ludwig Wittgenstein (1958) suggested a family resemblance approach in situations like this (his original example had to do with the difficulty of defining the word *game*). Just as no two members of a family look exactly alike yet bear a sufficient family resemblance to allow discerning strangers to recognise them as belonging to the same family, so also we can decide whether two texts belong to the same genre by identifying a family resemblance in terms of shared communicative purpose.

Finally, as with families, genres belong in networks of related texts. Abstracts, for instance, form a network with conference papers, research articles and theses. Shampoo labels in turn form a network with advertisements and other texts that shampoo companies use to promote their brand. Once again, the labels that people use to identify genres can offer insight into the larger network, or macro genre that a genre belongs to. Genre labels can also help us identify hybrid genres resulting from genre blending such as *edutainment* (education delivered in an entertainment format) and *advertorials* (advertisements adopting the form of editorials). Keep in mind that every genre has its own set of norms, which both enable and constrain design choices affecting the selection, sequencing and styling of a genre's content.

Activity 2.4

Genre labels tend to highlight their communicative purpose, but can also emphasise form, content, media format and target audience. Can you group the genre labels below, based on the aspect of the genre that the label highlights?

report	*poem*	*adventure*	*phone-in*
lecture	*letter*	*blog*	*western*
review	*sms*	*story*	*sci-fi*
cartoon	*romance*	*email*	*commentary*

A possible answer to Activity 2.4

PURPOSE	FORM	CONTENT	MEDIA
report	poem	adventure	blog
lecture	letter	western	phone-in
review	cartoon	romance	SMS
commentary	story	sci-fi	email

Activity 2.5

What formal and functional aspects of the parent genres do these hybrid genres reflect?
infomercial   docudrama   mockumentary   dramedy

Activity 2.6

Write down as many genre labels as you can. Now, try to group the labels, using the categories from Activity 2.4. If you think you need more categories, go ahead and create them, as long as you justify the need for each.

Activity 2.7

Based on what you've learnt about genres and norms, does the wedding invitation on the next page strike you as odd — why (not)? Answer clearly, concisely and coherently in 300 words or less.

YOU ARE REGRETFULLY INVITED
TO THE WEDDING BETWEEN MY PERFECT SON,

The Doctor

AND SOME

Cheap Two-Bit Tramp

WHOSE NAME ESCAPES ME RIGHT NOW.

THE BIGGEST DISASTER IN MY
FAMILY'S HISTORY WILL TAKE PLACE AT

9pm on Saturday, September 8th

AND NO DOUBT END IN DIVORCE.
HOPEFULLY IN TIME TO STILL BE ELIGIBLE FOR AN ANNULMENT.
THE OVERWHELMINGLY DISAPPOINTING HEARTBREAK OF A CEREMONY
WILL BE FOLLOWED BY DINNER, WHERE NUTS WILL BE SERVED
BECAUSE WHATSHERFACE HAS AN ALLERGY.

Retrieved May 1, 2012 from
http://www.etiquettehell.com/smf/index.php?topic=19729.0;prev_next=prev

References

Bazerman, Charles. (1988). *Shaping Written Knowledge: The genre and activity of the experimental article in science*. Madison: University of Wisconsin Press.

Bazerman, Charles. (1997). The life of genre, the life in the classroom. In W. Bishop and H. Ostrum (Eds.) *Genre and Writing*. Portsmouth, NH: Boynton/Cook, pp. 19-26.

Booth, Wayne C. (2005). Blind skepticism versus a rhetoric of assent. *College English, 67*(4), 378–388.

Brockriede, Wayne. (1975/1990). Where is argument? In R. Trapp & J. Schuetz (Eds.) *Perspectives on Argumentation: Essays in honor of Wayne Brockriede*. Illinois: Waveland Press, pp.4-8.

Crider, Scott F. (2005). *The Office of Assertion: An art of rhetoric for the academic essay*. Wilmington, Delaware: ISI Books.

Goodnight, Thomas. (1982). The personal, technical and public spheres of argument: a speculative inquiry into the art of public deliberation. *Journal of American Forensic Association 18*, 214-227.

Hymes, Dell. (1972). Models of the interaction of language and social life. In J. Gumperz and D. Hymes (Eds.), *Directions in Sociolinguistics: The ethnography of communication*. New York: Holt, Rinehart & Winston, pp.35-71.

Inch, Edward S. and Warnick, Barbara. (2010). *Critical Thinking and Communication: The use of reason in argument* (6th edition). Boston: Allyn & Bacon.

Jacobs, Scott and Jackson, Scott. (1982). Conversational argument: A discourse analytic approach. In J.R. Cox & C.A Willard (eds.) *Advances in Argumentation Theory and Research*. Southern Illinois University Press.

Martin, James R. (1985). Process and text: Two aspects of human semiosis. In J.D. Benson & W.S. Greaves (Eds.) *Systemic Perspectives in Discourse, Vol. 1* Norwood, NJ: Ablex, 248-274.

Miller, Carolyn R. (1984). Genre as social action. *Quarterly Journal of Speech 70*,151-167.

Selzer, John. (2004). Rhetorical analysis: Understanding how texts persuade readers. In C. Bazerman & P. Prior (eds.) *What Writing Does and How it Does it: An introduction to analysing texts and textual practices*. NJ: Lawrence Erlbaum, pp.279-307.

Schryer, Catherine F. (1993). Records as Genre. *Written Communication 10*(2), 200-234.

Swales, John. (1990). *Genre Analysis: English in academic and research settings*. Cambridge: Cambridge University Press.

Swales, John. (2004). *Research Genres: Explorations and applications*. Cambridge: Cambridge University Press.

Wenzel, Joseph. (1990). Three Perspectives on Argument: Rhetoric, Dialectic, Logic. In R. Trapp & J. Schuetz (Eds.) *Perspectives on Argumentation: Essays in Honor of Wayne Brockriede*. Illinois: Waveland Press, pp.9-26.

Wittgenstein, Ludwig. (1958). *Philosophical Investigations*. Oxford: Basil Blackwell.

Chapter 3 Participants

What roles can the addresser play?

What roles can the audience play?

How can we analyse the relationship between addressers and audiences?

How can speech act theory and politeness theory aid rhetorical analysis?

3.1   Addresser roles: principal, author, animator

In chapter 2, we considered *situation, norms* and *genres* in Hymes's (1972) SPEAKING mnemonic. In this chapter, we consider the *participants* in a communicative activity. The **addresser** is the person conveying the message, and the **addressee** is the intended audience of the message. When we talk to ourselves, we perform both roles, just like an actor performing different roles in a one-person stage show. Some communication models use the terms *sender* and *receiver*, but I prefer the terms *addresser* and *addressee* for two reasons.

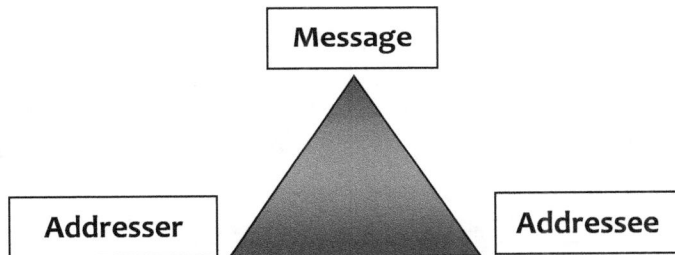

Figure 3.1   The communication triangle

First, the term *addressee* conveys the meaning of *intended audience* which the term *receiver* does not. Think about times when you've received a letter addressed to someone else or a message that you were asked to pass on. Suppose your mother asks you to tell your brother that dinner is ready. You receive the message that dinner is ready, knowing that its intended audience, or addressee, is your brother. What we have here is an example of **mediated communication** with you functioning as the intermediary between your mother and brother.

Social anthropologist Erving Goffman (1981) viewed communication as a theatrical performance, and distinguished three main roles that addressers can perform:

❖ the **principal** is the source of the message, "the party whose position, stand, and belief the words attest" (p.226).

❖ the **author** is "the agent who puts together, composes or scripts the lines that are uttered" (*ibid*); and,

❖ the **animator** is the voice-box, "the sounding box from which the utterances come" (*ibid*).

An addresser can perform all three roles. For example, if I were to conceptualise, compose and deliver a public lecture expressing my views on argument, then I would be the principal, author and animator of my message. But, principals (the individuals or groups wishing to convey a message) can also outsource the roles of author and animator to others.

A shampoo advertisement on television is likely employ such a division of labour, in that the principal (the shampoo brand that wants its product advertised) hires authors (copywriters who design the shampoo advertisement) who in turn hire animators (actors who perform the shampoo advertisement, whether as voice-over announcers, characters speaking to camera or characters enacting the advertisement's storyline). This division of addresser roles is typical in collaboratively-produced institutional and media discourses like political speeches, corporate reports, press releases and public service announcements.

Activity 3.1

Prof A has a sore throat. So, she turns to the student sitting next to her and says, *Ilyas, would you please tell the class they can take their 15-minute class break now?* How might Ilyas convey Prof A's message to his classmates? For each version that you come up with, state which addresser roles (principal, author, animator), Ilyas is performing, explaining your reasoning, clearly and concisely.

Comment on Activity 3.1

Ilyas: *Class, Prof A says we can take our 15-minute class break now.*
Ilyas attributes the message *we can take our 15-minute class break now* to Prof A, making clear that he is functioning as her spokesman. In Goffman's terms, Ilyas is the animator, since he delivers Prof A's message almost verbatim, making Prof A the principal and author of Ilyas's utterance.

Ilyas: *Hey, guys, break-time! Be back in 15, please!*
Ilyas doesn't attribute his announcement to Prof A or parrot her words, making him the author and animator of the announcement. He is not, however, the principal, since it was Prof A and not Ilyas who wanted the announcement made.

3.2   Addressee roles: who's the decision maker?

In section 2.7, we saw how Aristotle distinguished three genres of rhetoric:

> The genres of rhetoric are three in number, which is the number of the types of audience. For a speech is composed of three factors—the speaker, the subject, and the listener—and it is to the last of these that its purpose is related. Now the listener must be either a spectator or a judge, and, if a judge, one either of the past or the future. The judge, then about the future is the assembly member, the judge about the past is the juror, and the assessor of capacity is the spectator, so that there must needs be three types of rhetorical speech: *deliberative, forensic* and *display.*
>
> (Aristotle, 1356b, p. 80)

Aristotle talks about speakers and listeners rather than readers and writers in the excerpt above because classical Greek rhetoric prioritised public oratory. Aristotle saw the audience's role as that of judge or assessor. What varied was the nature of the thing being judged, as summarised in Figure 3.2.

Genre	Audience	What is judged
Deliberative	assembly members	future action
Forensic	jurors	past action
Epideictic	spectators	present action

Figure 3.2   How Aristotle saw the audience's role

Contemporary rhetoricians Richard Young, Alton Becker and Kenneth Pike (1970) in turn ask WHO does the judging, the arguers themselves or a third-party audience, distinguishing between **dyadic** and **triadic arguments** (see Figure 3.3).

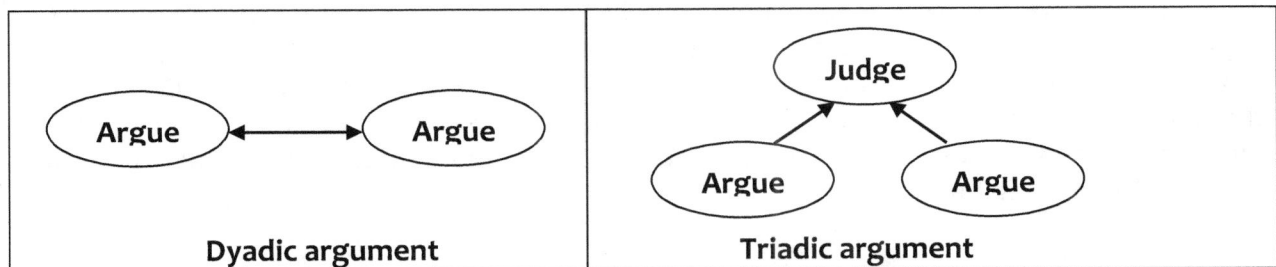

Figure 3.3   Dyadic and triadic arguments

Dyadic argument refers to two-way argument, in which arguers talk directly to each other, trying to influence each other's beliefs, attitudes and behaviour. The arguers are also the judges in that each must decide whether and how far to assent to what the other is saying. In contrast, **triadic argument** involves a three-way interaction, in which the arguers don't address each other. Instead, they make their case to an impartial third-party who serves as judge, weighing up the merits of each case.

Aristotle discussed triadic rather than dyadic argument, which perhaps explains why most people think of argument as an adversarial exchange, in which two rhetors lock horns over an issue in order to be judged victorious by an impartial third-party audience. The best known-example of this adversarial process is the criminal trial, where prosecutor and defence attorney present their case to impartial jurors who decide which case is more convincing. In academic debate competitions, similarly, each team presents its case, leaving it to the judge(s) to decide which case (affirmative or negative) was more compelling.

Edward Inch and Barbara Warnick (2010) refer to the addressees in triadic arguments as "third-party audiences" (p.192) because the decision-makers are not the arguers themselves but a third-party. In personal sphere arguments (see section 2.8), the third-party audience may be someone whom the arguers have chosen. For example, if you live in a hall of residence, and you and your roommate cannot resolve an argument by yourselves, you may turn to a trusted resident advisor or staff member to adjudicate. In technical and public sphere arguments, the third-party audience typically comprises one or more experts assigned to the case by the relevant institutional body. The process of arbitration is a prime example, involving as it does an impartial third-party assigned to weigh the merits of each case before rendering a legally-binding decision.

3.3   Power differential and social distance

Regardless of whether we're analysing dyadic or triadic arguments, we need a way to understand the relationship between addressers and addressees. Discourse analysts typically analyse this relationship along two dimensions, power differential (the hierarchical distance between the participants in terms of status and rank) and social distance (how well the participants know each other).

The two dimensions represent two intersecting clines. **Social distance** is measured along a horizontal cline ranging from very close (e.g. intimate friends) to very distant (complete strangers). **Power differential** in turn is measured along a vertical cline ranging from superior to inferior with egalitarian relationships in the centre. To visualise participant relations, discourse analysts plot the participants' social distance and power differential on the **X** and **Y** axes of a graph (see Figure 3.4, where **Z** represents the Addressee). The point at which the **X** and **Y** axes intersect represents a relationship among equals who are neither socially close nor distant.

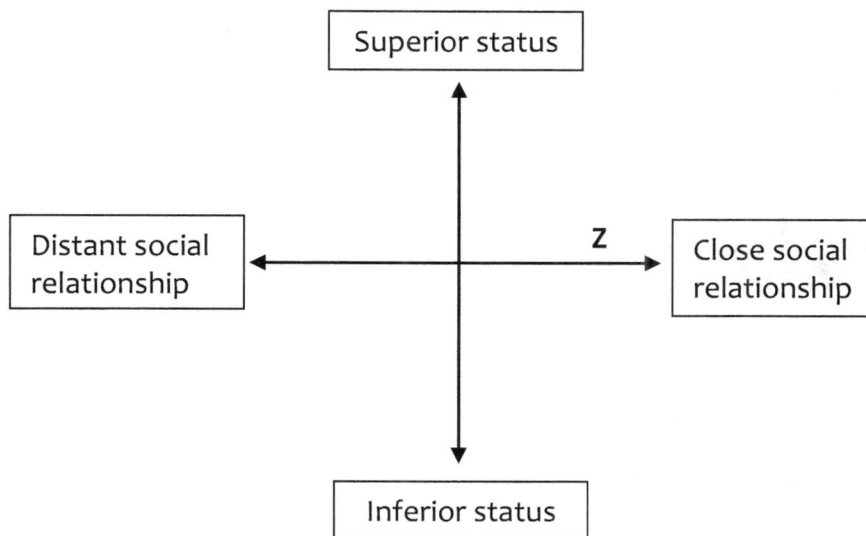

Figure 3.4   Power differential and social distance

Activity 3.2

Figure 3.4 shows the addressee **Z** to be someone whom the addresser feels close to, and considers slightly superior to herself. Who might **Z** be?

Comment on Activity 3.2

The addressee **Z** could be a parent, older sibling, teacher or employer. Here's my reasoning: In close-knit nuclear families, the social distance between siblings and parent-child tends to be minimal. So, based solely on the social distance axis, we might infer that **Z** is a family member. But, since the addresser considers **Z** to be slightly superior to herself, **Z** could be an older sibling or parent, assuming a traditional family dynamic in which elders are conferred greater social status and respect, ranking higher on the 'power' scale.

In a school setting, **Z** could be a teacher whom the addresser knows very well but considers slightly superior to herself, assuming an institutional hierarchy in which teachers rank higher than students.

A third possibility is that **Z** represents the boss in a work setting where employer and employee are on fairly intimate terms, but where the workers still perceive their boss as ranking higher than themselves in the workplace culture.

Obviously, these are not the only possibilities. So, be prepared to justify your own answers cogently, paying attention to both axes of the graph.

Discourse analysts pay close attention to participant relationships when analysing discourse because we don't talk the same way to everyone. In fact, we are so aware of the social nuances of language use that when we overhear an utterance without knowing the exact identity of the discourse participants, we are still able to draw reasonable inferences about their relative rank and social distance based on how they speak to each other.

Activity 3.3

Suppose you walked past a room without being able to see inside, and overheard a male voice utter the words *Oi, you, get off my chair!* What might you surmise about the relationship between addresser and addressee?

Comment on Activity 3.3

I'd infer that the addresser considers the addressee equal to or lower in status, based on a cultural norm that we don't tell our superiors what to do in bald imperatives. Politeness theory (see section 3.7) helps explain why we don't.

3.4   Knowing your audience

Real estate agents utter the mantra *Location, location, location*. Rhetors' equivalent mantra would be *Know your audience*. Knowing your audience may not be difficult in personal sphere arguments among family and close friends (see section 2.8). But, it can be a challenge in public and technical sphere arguments amongst (relative) strangers. Public sphere audiences tend to be more heterogeneous than technical and personal sphere audiences, comprising a mix of people with varied levels of knowledge, interest and support for the issue and rhetor. Public sphere arguments also tend to centre on controversial issues sparking strong emotion. Think, for instance, of long-standing public debates about abortion, capital punishment, euthanasia, human rights, etc.

The rhetorical perspective on argument recognises that human beings are not logic machines but sentient beings with deep-seated values about right and wrong, good and bad. Most argument textbooks advise students to begin their analysis of the audience by considering the audience's demographic characteristics as a proxy for discovering the audience's beliefs and attitudes towards the issue being argued. These demographic details typically include age, sex, sexual orientation, ethnic culture, socioeconomic status and education as well as political and religious affiliation, described in terms of a continuum, ranging from *conservative* on the far right through *centrist* in the middle to *radical* on the far left.

To some extent, this demographic approach to audience analysis traces back to Aristotle's four-fold taxonomy analysing the effect of **emotion** (e.g. anger, envy, jealousy, love, hate, fear, friendship, confidence, shame, guilt, pity, disgust), **habits** (virtues and vices), **age** (youth, prime and old age), and **fortune** (wealth and well-being) on how an audience thinks, feels and behaves. Aristotle's discussion was influenced by the Greek idea of the Golden Mean in that he saw youth and old age as diametrically opposed to the Golden Mean of prime. Whereas the young and the old were prone to excess, those in their prime are supposedly

> mid-way in character between [the old and the young], avoiding the excess, and neither greatly confident (for that would be rashness) nor excessively fearful,...neither trusting all men, nor trusting none, but rather judging according to the truth,...neither living for nobility alone nor for self-interest but for both, and neither tending to extravagance nor to meanness, but seeking a balance, and similarly in point of temper and desire, and showing moderation with courage and courage with moderation.
>
> (Aristotle, 1390b, p.177)

Whether or not we agree with Aristotle's remarks above, different audiences do have different interests and priorities, which colour their views, influencing the arguments they're likely to find compelling. As Hollihan and Baaske (2005) observe, "poor citizens may be inclined to support increased government spending on social programs to help provide for human needs, while affluent citizens may be motivated to cut such programs in order to keep their taxes as low as possible" (p.11). Similarly, "[o]ne body of readers — say a group of fraternity men may respond to a direct appeal in strong language; another group—say, members of a Methodist congregation—may reject your whole argument if you use a word like 'crap'" (McDonald, 1993, p.3).

3.5   Analysing the audience: friendlies, neutrals, hostiles

Persuasion consultant Harry Mills (2000, p.201) offers an alternative framework for audience analysis, focusing on three questions (see Figures 3.5 and 5.5).

Area	Question to be asked by rhetor
Knowledge	*How much does this audience know about (a) the issue and (b) me?*
Interest	*How interested are they in (a) the issue and (b) me?*
Support	*How much support already exists for (a) my view and (b) me?*

Figure 3.5   Analysing the audience's knowledge, interest and support

Mills assumes that audiences pay attention to both the issue and the rhetor, an idea consonant with persuasion viewed as a rhetorical triangle, comprising a trustworthy rhetor seeking to influence an audience's beliefs, attitudes and behaviour through a convincing message.

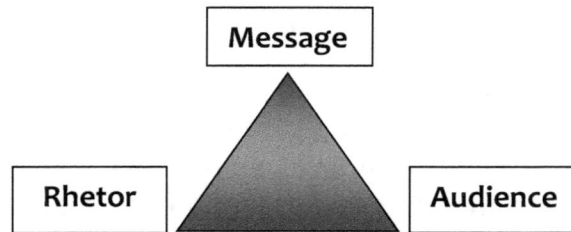

Figure 3.6   The rhetorical triangle

Mills (2000, p.200) suggests that based on the answers to the questions about the audience's level of knowledge, interest and support, we can generate six audience profiles (see Figure 3.7).

Audience Type	Characteristic
Hostile	disagrees with me, may be working actively against me
Neutral	understands my position but needs convincing
Uninterested	informed about the issue but not interested in it
Uninformed	lacks the information they need to be convinced
Supportive	already agrees with me
Mixed	holds a variety of attitudes towards the issue and me

Figure 3.7   Mills's (2000, p.200) six audience types

If this six-way profile seems a tad cumbersome to work with, we can conflate it into a simple three-way profile by envisaging members of an audience as belonging in one of three *knowing zones* (Mills, 2006, p.206) — the red zone of rejection, the yellow zone of noncommitment or the green zone of acceptance (see Figure 3.8).

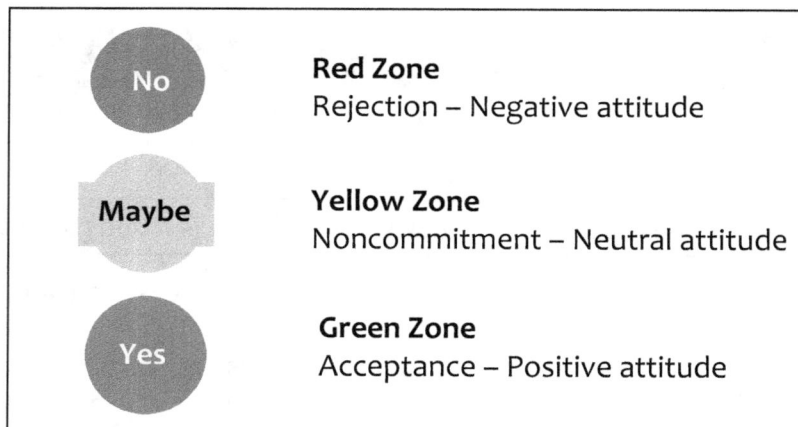

No   **Red Zone**
             Rejection – Negative attitude

Maybe   **Yellow Zone**
             Noncommitment – Neutral attitude

Yes   **Green Zone**
             Acceptance – Positive attitude

Figure 3.8   Mills's (2000, p.206) *knowing zones*

Audience analysis helps rhetors adapt the invention, organisation and style of their arguments to their audience. Aristotle identifies three types of **rhetorical appeals**, *logos*, *ethos* and *pathos*, corresponding to the three elements (message, rhetor and audience) of the rhetorical triangle (see Figure 3.9).

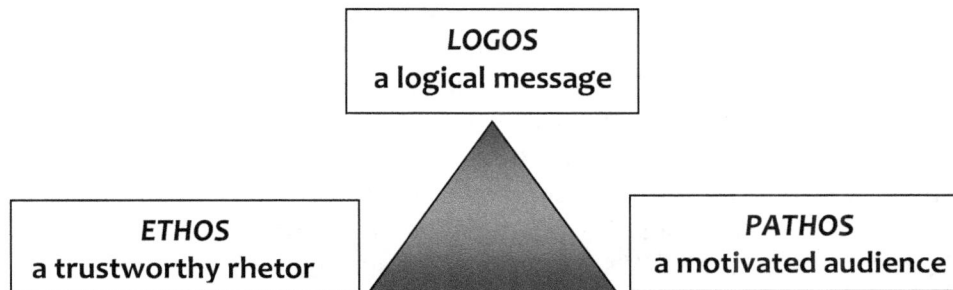

LOGOS
a logical message

ETHOS		PATHOS
a trustworthy rhetor		a motivated audience

Figure 3.9   **Three types of rhetorical appeals**

Aristotle's point is that convincing arguments employ appeals of logic, emotion and character, i.e. that people tend to find convincing those arguments made by rhetors whom they deem trustworthy, appealing to minds (reason) and hearts (emotions) alike (see section 4.9). The appeal of reason, or *logos*, stems from an expectation that the rhetor's message will be logical, since we want to know *beyond a reasonable doubt* (see section 1.3) that our beliefs, attitudes and behaviour rest on good reasons. But, logic on its own will not inspire action. For that, we need motivational appeals, or *pathos*, drawing from the rich depths of human emotion (e.g. fear and hope, love and hatred, anger and sorrow, pride and shame) to move us. But, the bedrock of persuasion, at least according to Aristotle, is the appeal of character, or *ethos*.

3.6   Analysing *ethos*

When analysing texts, it's important to distinguish the **text world**, the version of reality constructed by a rhetor's language use, from the **real world**, the world we physically inhabit. As children, we played cowboys and Indians, cops and robbers, doctor and patient, pretending to be characters in worlds of our imagining. RPGs, or role-playing games, are just the latest (digital) version of our human capacity for building alternative realities, with terms like *avatar* for the **persona**, or character mask or role assumed in the game world.

Long before the invention of computers, however, poets and story-tellers were adopting myriad **personas** as lovers and warriors, heroes and villains, to entertain and educate audiences of all ages. When we read novels, we distinguish the author of the work from the teller of the tale, or narrator. Similarly, when analysing *ethos*, we distinguish the (real-world) rhetor from the (text-world) persona constructed by the rhetor's words. Here is how Aristotle explains it:

> Persuasion is achieved by the speaker's personal character where the speech is so spoken as to make us think him credible. We believe good men more fully and

more readily than others; this is true generally whatever the question is, and absolutely true where exact certainty is impossible and opinions are divided. *This kind of persuasion, like the others, should be achieved by what the speaker says, not by what people think of his character before he begins to speak.*

(*Rhetoric* 1356a, cited in Inch and Warnick, 2010, p.202, italics mine)

Inch and Warnick (2010) highlight three key points about *ethos* (trustworthiness). First, *ethos* is something that the audience imputes to the rhetor because "the speech is so spoken as to make us think him credible" (p.202). In other words, *ethos* derives from the persona performed by the rhetor in the persuasion message. Inch and Warnick (2010) distinguish between initial and derived credibility. Initial credibility stems from "an arguer's credentials, status, and reputation as known to recipients *before* they hear or read the message" (p.203, emphasis mine). *Ethos*, however, refers to *derived credibility* (p.203), *derived* from WHAT a rhetor says and HOW s/he says it (see section 2.6).

Second, *ethos* is crucial to persuasion because "where certainty is impossible... opinions are divided" (Inch and Warnick, 2010, p.202) and when we're unable to verify things for ourselves, we're forced to rely on the word of others. And, we are more likely, as Aristotle observes, to trust the word of those who demonstrate good sense, good will and good character:

> (1) Good sense relates to the ability to display that one is 'intelligent'. (2) Good character relates to the fact that the identity that one is displaying radiates positive values such as honesty, sincerity and so on, which can be directly linked to Linde's observations that "people do not want just any objectifiable self; they want a good self, and a self that is perceived as good by others" (Linde, 1993:122). (3) Goodwill relates to the fact that the displayed identity has the interlocutor's concerns at heart.

(Clifton & van de Mieroop, 2010, 2450-1)

Contemporary rhetoricians in turn see *ethos* (trustworthiness) as stemming from **expertise** (*good sense*) and **integrity** (*good will* and *good character*).

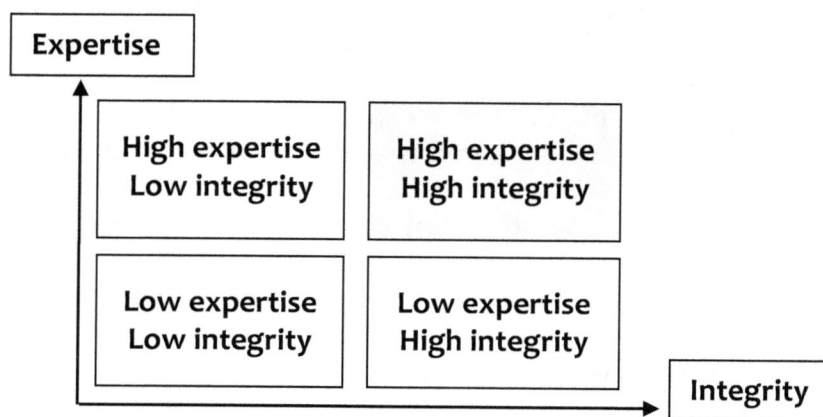

Figure 3.10   **Trustworthiness = Expertise + Integrity**

Third, *ethos* (our impression of the rhetor's trustworthiness) ebbs and flows both within and across texts because texts are dynamic rhetorical performances. Openings and closings are critically important locations for doing *ethos* because of the *primacy-recency effect* (Bostrom, 1983, p.178) — the discovery that people tend to remember what comes first or last. A **primacy effect** occurs when information presented first has greater impact, while a **recency effect** occurs when information presented last has greater impact (see section 4.6).

3.7 *Ethos* and politeness

One way rhetors do *ethos* is to adhere to politeness norms. Perhaps the best known work on politeness is Penelope Brown and Stephen Levinson's (1987) attempt to construct a universal theory of politeness, based on conversational data ranging from English and Japanese to Tzeltal and Tamil. Central to their theory is the idea of face (the public self-image we wish to claim), inspired by Goffman's (1967) concept of **face work**, deriving from the Chinese notion of face.

Brown and Levinson's (1987) concept of face comprises two kinds of desires, or **face wants** that all language users attribute to one another:

❖ **Positive face**: the claim to a positive self-image approved of by others

❖ **Negative face**: "the basic claim to territories, personal preserves, rights to non-distraction, i.e. to freedom of action and freedom from imposition" (p.61).

Positive and negative face wants represent opposing demands for communality and independence. And, since communicative activity typically involves two or more participants, **politeness norms** require us to manage the positive- and negative-face wants of our interlocutors and ourselves.

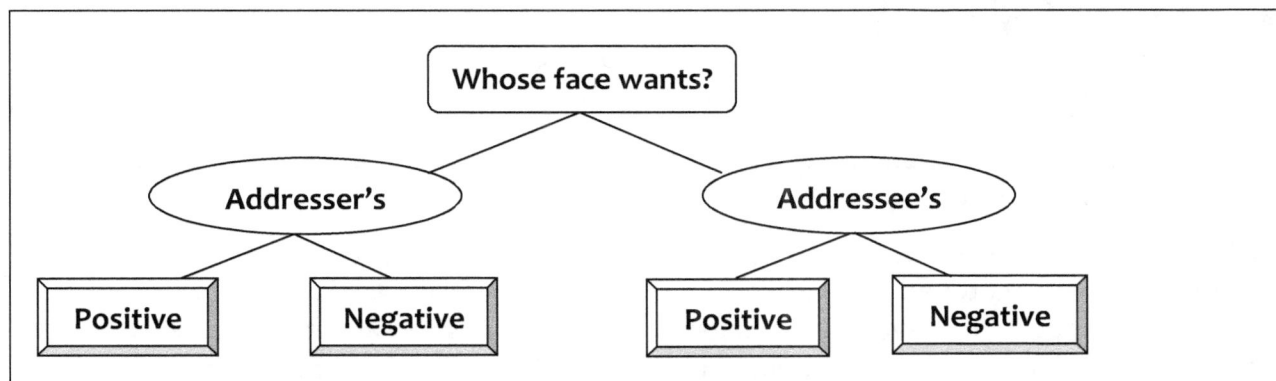

Figure 3.11   A heuristic for analysing face work

Face can be saved, maintained, enhanced and threatened. According to Brown and Levinson (1987), all social groups have evolved politeness strategies as a way of mitigating or redressing face threatening acts (FTAs). Positive-politeness strategies mitigate or redress threats to positive face (our desire to be approved of), while negative-politeness strategies mitigate and redress threats to negative face (our desire not to be imposed on).

Positive-politeness strategies seek to emphasise solidarity by

- ❖ avoiding disagreement,
- ❖ identifying with an addressee's point of view
- ❖ using in-group identity markers such as dialect, jargon and slang,
- ❖ giving compliments, and
- ❖ demonstrating reciprocity.

Negative-politeness strategies in turn recognise that we all want our freedom of action unhindered and our attention unimpeded. Brown and Levinson (1987) explain that "negative-politeness strategies consist in assurances that the speaker recognizes and respects the addressee's negative-face wants and will not (or will only minimally) interfere with the addressee's freedom of action" (p. 70). Negative-politeness strategies minimise imposition by, among other things,

- ❖ indicating pessimism about a request being granted (e.g. *I don't suppose I could borrow your ruler for just a minute*)
- ❖ giving interlocutors options so that they don't feel coerced,
- ❖ apologizing,
- ❖ showing deference, and
- ❖ impersonalising directives (e.g. *Patrons are requested to switch off their mobile phones*).

Activity 3.4

Your friend Bill asks to borrow twenty dollars from you. Whose face and which face wants are potentially threatened?

Comment on Activity 3.4

Bill's (positive and negative) face and your (positive and negative) face are threatened: Bill's positive face is threatened because he must now see himself as someone who bothers others with requests for favours. His negative face in turn is threatened because he has to admit to himself that he's not independent but dependent on you for the twenty dollars he's just asked to borrow. Your negative face, meanwhile, is threatened because your freedom to act is curtailed by the knowledge that Bill probably expects you to grant his request out of solidarity (his hope that you care enough to help him out) or reciprocity (if he has done you comparable favours). If you reject Bill's request, you damage your own positive face because you're now the kind of person who denies a friend in need. Do note that answers may vary, depending on cultural norms of friendship.

Figuring out what kinds of acts threaten face and who has special rights to face protection can be tricky because cultures vary in terms of the relative value they place on different kinds of politeness strategies. In American culture, for example, it's generally considered polite to offer guests a choice of refreshments, whereas in Japanese culture, this would be perceived as imposing the burden of choice on one's guest, and the polite thing to do would be to just go ahead and serve tea.

Activity 3.5

How would you enhance the politeness of this email? Justify your revision, clearly, concisely and coherently.

Hi Professor Abraham,

Attached is our project proposal. Please read it because we will be coming to see you At 6:30 pm today to ask you some questions about our project.

3.8   Speech act theory: *saying is doing*

Speech act theory was developed by philosophers of language John Austin (1962) and John Searle (1976) in recognition of the fact that when we speak, we are not only *saying* something but also *doing* something because all utterances convey a meaning, possess a force, and elicit an effect. Austin (1962) and Searle (1976) refer to the meaning-form configuration of an utterance as its *locution*. *Illocution* in turn refers to the force that an utterance possesses by virtue of the addresser's intention in making the utterance. And, *perlocution* refers to the message uptake or effect elicited on the addressee by the utterance.

The distinction between **illocution** and **perlocution** highlights the gap between purpose and outcome, or intention and effect, reminding us that communication involves inferring what a speaker means (subtext) based on interpreting what the speaker says (text) in context (see Figure 3.12).

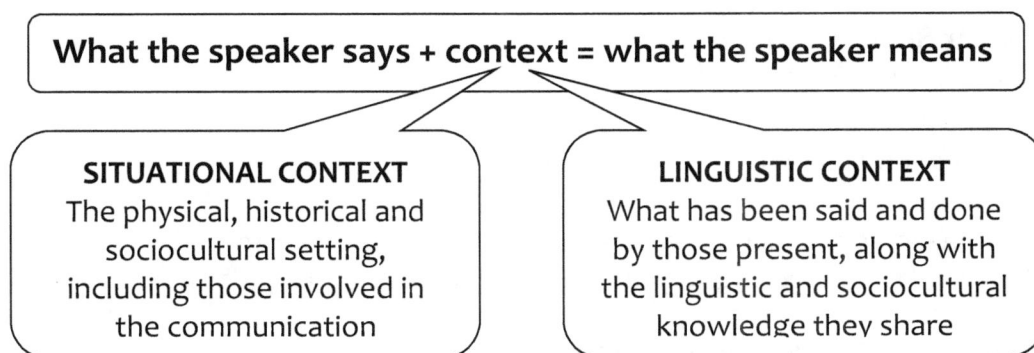

Figure 3.12   Interpreting text in context

Activity 3.6

If your best friend said *I'll never speak to you again*, how would you report this utterance? Would you choose (a), (b) or neither, and why?

(a)   My best friend threatened never to speak to me again.

(b)   My best friend promised never to speak to me again.

Austin (1962) and Searle (1976) labelled speech acts, based on their illocution (speaker's intention), and among the speech acts studied by linguists, six have received particular attention (see Figure 3.13).

Speech act	Defining characteristic
Representative	*Addresser asserts a true/false belief about the world*
Verdictive	*Addresser judges something to be good or bad*
Expressive	*Addresser expresses his/her inner (psychological) state*
Declaration	*Addresser brings about change in the world via utterance*
Commissive	*Addresser commits to doing something*
Directive	*Addresser wants addressee to do something*

Figure 3.13   Six types of speech acts

Representatives are so-named because they represent speakers' beliefs about the world, whose truth can be verified empirically or analytically. Examples of representatives include assertions about past, present and future events, including recounts, descriptions and predictions.

Examples of Representatives
It rained all day yesterday.
It's raining right now.
It will rain again tomorrow.

Verdictives are speech acts which judge the value of something. Examples of verdictives include the acts of ranking, assessing, appraising and condoning. The judgment of quality in verdictive speech acts is conveyed through evaluative words and phrases, reflecting a positive or negative value judgment. Let's clarify the difference between representatives and verdictives with an example. Compare utterances (a) and (b):

(a) *Persuasion* is a novel.   (b) *Persuasion* is a masterful novel.

Utterance (a) is a representative speech act because it asserts a true/false belief about the world, namely the speaker's belief about the literary genre of *Persuasion* — that it is a novel (and not, say, a poem, short story, or essay). Since we have a shared system for categorising literary works, we can check the accuracy of sentence (a) fairly easily. In contrast, sentence (b) is a verdictive speech act because it renders a verdict (*masterful*) judging the quality of the novel, measured against some aesthetic standard.

Activity 3.7

State what is being judged in the verdictives below, clearly identifying the words conveying the positive or negative evaluation.

1. *Joel played that sonata really well.*

2. *Sarah wrote an outstanding essay.*

3. *Your argument failed to persuade us.*

Answers to Activity 3.7

1. Joel's playing of the sonata is judged positively, as conveyed by the adverbial phrase *really well*.

2. Sarah's essay is judged positively, as conveyed by the adjective *outstanding*.

3. The addressee's argument is judged negatively, as conveyed by the verb phrase *failed to persuade*.

Activity 3.8

How would you categorise the following speech acts?

(1) *Jennifer is a sex worker.*   (2) *Jennifer is a slut.*

Comment on Activity 3.8

I'd categorise (1) as a representative and (2) as a verdictive because *sex worker* is a value-neutral term for me, whereas *slut*, with its extremely negative connotation, seems to be judging Jennifer's lack of moral fitness.

Expressives are so-named because they express speakers' internal or psychological states, i.e. their hopes and fears, wishes and desires. Greetings, apologies, congratulations, condolences and giving thanks are all examples of expressives. Let's clarify the difference between expressives and representatives with an example.

(c) I feel drunk.　　　　　　　　(d) I am drunk.

Utterance (c) is an expressive because the verb *feels* conveys information about the speaker's inner world, which only s/he is privy to, given that we can't see inside another person's mind. In contrast, utterance (d) is a representative because the verb *am* introduces a claim whose truth can be empirically verified, e.g. by having the speaker blow into a breathalyser or take a blood test.

Examples of Expressives

I'm so sorry for your loss.　　　　　*Congratulations on your promotion!*
Thank you for your lovely card.

The fourth type of speech act in Figure 3.13, **declarations,** bring about the state of affairs declared in the utterance, but only if the right person says the right words at the right time in the right *setting* and *scene*. In other words, to properly perform a declaration, the speaker must have the appropriate institutional authority in the given context. For example, the utterance *I hereby pronounce you husband and wife* has the effect of turning two single people into husband and wife *if and only if* it is uttered by a licensed agent of the state during a wedding ceremony. Examples of declarations include blessings, baptisms, hirings, firings, resignations, arrests and dismissals.

Examples of Declarations

Minister of Arts:　　*I hereby declare this exhibition open.*

Presiding judge:　　*Case dismissed.*

Police officer:　　*You're under arrest.*

The final two speech acts in Figure 3.13, commissives and directives, both involve action, but differ in terms of who's responsible for carrying out the action — speaker or addressee. With commissives, it is the speaker who commits to doing the stated action (e.g. *I promise never to steal again.*) whereas in directives, it is the addressee who's required to carry out the specified action (e.g. *Promise me you will never steal again*).

Threats, promises, refusals, vows and pledges are all examples of **commissives**. Speakers can use **performative verbs** (verbs that name the action being performed) such as *swear, promise, vow, pledge* or *commit* to convey their commitment explicitly. Equally, they can commit to an action, using a verb phrase comprising the modal verb *will* (as opposed to the more tentative *may* or *could*) followed by an action verb, as illustrated below.

Examples of Commissives

I promise to love you in sickness and in health.
I will find you.　　　　*I will never visit them again.*

Directives in turn include commands, requests, challenges, invitations, entreaties and dares. And, speakers can use **performative verbs** such as *order, request, beg, plead* and *permit* or *let us* (which highlights solidarity between speaker and addressee) to make their directive intention explicit.

Examples of Directives

Please switch off the lights when you leave.

Let us pray.   *What time is it, please?*

3.9   Direct and indirect speech acts

When analysing speech acts, it's important to distinguish form from function (see Figure 3.14), since one form can have multiple functions, and *vice versa*.

FORM	Example	Typical FUNCTION
Declarative	*She went away.*	conveying information
Interrogative	*Did she go away?*	seeking information
Imperative	*Go away.*	issuing commands
Exclamatory	*How rude!*	expressing attitudes

Figure 3.14   Four kinds of English sentences

To perform a directive speech act, a speaker could select the imperative form *Lend me your ruler* or the interrogative form *Will you lend me your ruler?* Each design choice will influence a speaker's *ethos*. The question *Will you lend me your ruler?* mitigates the threat to the addressee's negative face by giving him/her a measure of choice, unlike the bald imperative *Lend me your ruler*.

Deciding which form is preferable depends on the **social distance** and **power differential** between addresser and addressee, and how each sees the **weight of the imposition** placed on the addressee. These three factors help addressers calibrate the politeness strategies used: the greater the weight of the imposition, the larger the power differential and the further the social distance between addresser and addressee, the more polite the exchange will tend to be.

To mitigate the imposition inherent to directives, speakers typically use **politeness formulas** like *please, thank you* and *with all due respect* within **indirect speech acts** (see Activity 3.9). Similarly, to mitigate the inherent threat in verdictives of imposing one's judgment on another, addressers typically use **indirect speech acts** coupled with **hedges** or **boosters** (words and phrases aimed at qualifying or amplifying evaluative statements).

Activity 3.9

Janet is speaking to her good friend Richard. Rank Janet's utterances below in terms of politeness, clearly explaining your reasoning.

(1)   *Could we watch a movie tonight?*

(2)   *I'd love it if you would watch a movie with me tonight.*

(3)   *It would be nice if we could watch a movie tonight.*

Comment on Activity 3.9

I would rank (1) as the most polite because it is clear without being coercive, followed by (3) and (2), respectively.

Utterance (1) makes clear what Janet wants Richard to do, but mitigates the threat to Richard's negative face by couching a directive as a *Yes/No question* offering Richard some choice in the matter.

Utterances (2) and (3) similarly give Richard a choice via the dependent clauses *if you would watch a movie with me tonight* and *if we could watch a movie tonight*, respectively. Both (2) and (3) are indirect speech acts, directives disguised as an expressive and a verdictive (Janet judges the movie-watching experience positively through the adjective *nice*), respectively.

Utterance (3) is more polite than (2) as it employs the negative-politeness strategy of impersonalising the request. In contrast, the strong verb *love* in (2) lets Richard know that if he were to turn Janet down, he would be denying her what she would *love* to do.

Do bear in mind that my answer reflects my norms. Argue your analysis, keeping an open mind as you listen to your friends' analyses. Consider, too, whether you ranked the three utterances the same way I did but for different reasons.

The notion of face work helps us explain why there are preferred and dispreferred responses to particular speech acts. For example, when someone invites you to a party, the **preferred response** would be acceptance rather than rejection of the invitation. We now have the tools to explain this asymmetry. By inviting you to the party, the inviter is showing his/ her approval of you, and expecting you to reciprocate. Accepting the invitation shows mutual goodwill and maintains the inviter's and your own positive face wants. In contrast, if you were to reject the invitation, you would be denying the inviter this demonstration of reciprocity. This explains why people typically apologise and explain their reasons for rejecting invitations, in order to redress the threat to the inviter's positive face, e.g.

Hugo: *Will you come to my birthday party on the 12th of June?*

Selma: *I'm so sorry. I would have loved to, but I'm in Taiwan all of June.*

Being communicatively competent involves inferring what a speaker intends or means, even when addressers use indirect speech acts. For example, if your boss says *Could you stop by my office at 11 am today?*, she is not issuing an invitation but an order couched as a request (cf. the bald imperative *Come by my office at 11 am today*).

To recap, politeness is pertinent to *ethos* because all rhetors have to adopt a persona (see section 3.6) which allows them to manage their own as well as their audience's face needs (see section 7.4). Aristotle's observation that we tend to respond well to people who "take our interests seriously", who "praise our good qualities", and who "will see not the bad, but the good in us" (*Rhetoric*, ii, 3-4, cited in Lunsford 1979, p.149) resonates with Brown and Levinson's (1987) notion of positive face needs. Politeness theory also helps explain the proscription against name-calling or projecting negative intentions onto others, when we argue, since that would threaten their positive and negative face wants. In order to persuade anyone, the rhetor's first task is to get people to stop and pay attention. And, people are far more likely to listen to us, if we show that we respect and value what they have to say. How rhetors create rapport with their audience is a theme we revisit in the remaining chapters of the book, as we consider how arguers invent, organise and style their arguments in response to audiences and issues.

References

Aristotle. *The Art of Rhetoric.* (1991). Translated with an introduction and notes by Hugo Lawson-Tancred. Harmondsworth: Penguin Classics.

Austin, John L. (1962). *How To Do Things With Words.* New York: Oxford University Press.

Bostrom, Robert N. (1983). *Persuasion.* Englewood Cliffs, NJ: Prentice-Hall.

Brown, Penelope. and Levinson, Stephen C. (1987). *Politeness: Some universals in language use.* Cambridge: Cambridge University Press.

Goffman, Erving. (1967). *Interaction Ritual: Essays on face-to-face behavior.* Allen Lane: The Penguin Press.

Goffman, Erving (1981). *Forms of Talk.* Philadelphia: University of Pennsylvania Press.

Hymes, Dell. (1972). Models of the interaction of language and social life. In J. Gumperz and D. Hymes (Eds.), *Directions in Sociolinguistics: The ethnography of communication.* New York: Holt, Rinehart & Winston, pp.35-71.

Inch, Edward S. and Warnick, Barbara (2010). *Critical Thinking And Communication: The use of reason in argument* (6th edition). Boston: Allyn & Bacon.

Lunsford, Andrea. (1979). Aristotelian vs. Rogerian argument A reassessment. *College Composition and Communication 30* (2), pp.146-151.

McDonald, Daniel. (1993). *The Language of Argument* (7th edition). New York: HarperCollins College Publishers.

Mills, Harry. (2000). *Artful Persuasion: How to command attention, change minds, and influence people.* New York: AMACOM.

Searle, John R. (1976). The classification of illocutionary acts. *Language in Society 5*(1), 1-24.

Young, Richard E., Becker Alton L., and Pike, Kenneth L. (1970). *Rhetoric: Discovery and change.* New York: Harcourt, Brace and World.

Chapter 4 Invention

What are the five canons of rhetoric?

How can stasis theory and Aristotle's topics help with invention?

How can logos, pathos and ethos be resources for invention?

What are the stock issues of policy argument?

4.1 The five canons of rhetoric

When rhetoric entered Greek life in the fifth century BC alongside the emergence of Greek democracy, Athenian politicians quickly recognised that success in oratory was too important a matter to be left to chance. Thus, "rhetorical training rapidly came to be in effect the equivalent of a modern university degree for those who sought prominence in Athenian public life" (Lawson-Tancred, 1991 p.4). It was in this context that Aristotle wrote his treatise on rhetoric, proposing his five canons of rhetoric (invention, organisation, style, memory and delivery), which the classical Roman orators Cicero (106-43 BC) and Quintilian (35-100 AD) developed to help rhetors select, sequence and style their arguments in response to specific audience and issues (see Figure 4.1).

Canon of rhetoric	Focus
Invention *What shall I say?*	selecting the arguments best suited to audience and rhetorical purpose
Organisation *How shall I organise what I want to say?*	sequencing arguments in the best order. Classical oratory comprised: • Exordium (introducing the argument) • Narration (forecasting the argument) • Confirmation (developing support for the claim) • Refutation (responding to objections) • Peroration (concluding the argument)
Style *How shall I express what I want to say?*	selecting the best language. Classical rhetoric employed *tropes* (marked lexis) and *schemes* (marked syntax)
Memory *How shall I remember what I want to say?*	using mnemonic devices to aid recall of what's been invented, organised and styled
Delivery *How shall I deliver my text?*	presenting the argument, drawing on • intonation, gesture & body language (oral discourse) • authorial voice and tone (written discourse)

Figure 4.1   The five canons of rhetoric

Classical rhetoric was primarily oral in nature, which explains the presence of the canons of memory and delivery in Figure 4.1. And, oratory continues to be an important skill, taught in classrooms devoted to public speaking. Max Atkinson's (2004) book *Lend me your ears: All you need to know about making speeches and presentations* offers an accessible linguistically-informed introduction to the subject, which I invite you to browse. Since our object of inquiry is argument rather than oratory, I focus on the canons common to both written and oral argument, namely the canons of invention, organisation and style. In this chapter, we explore invention, devoting the next two chapters to organisation and style in turn.

4.2 Aristotle's genres of rhetoric revisited

As outlined in sections 2.7 and 3.2, Aristotle distinguished three genres of rhetoric (forensic, deliberative and epideictic), based on communicative purpose. **Epideictic rhetoric** is displayed at ceremonial occasions (hence the alternative labels *ceremonial or display rhetoric*) and seeks to reinforce communal identity, by celebrating heroes and condemning common enemies.

One of the best known literary examples of epideictic rhetoric is Mark Antony's speech in Act 3, Scene 2 of Shakespeare's play *Julius Caesar*, which begins *Friends, Romans, countrymen, lend me your ears; / I come to bury Caesar, not to praise him*. Eulogies and commemoration speeches are good examples of display oratory as are their written counterparts, the condolence letter and farewell note. Other genres of epideictic rhetoric include award and medal citations as well as inauguration addresses, valedictory and victory speeches, all of which serve to reinforce communal values.

In Aristotle's time, **forensic rhetoric** was set in the courtroom (hence, its alternative label *judicial rhetoric*) and focused on questions of truth about past actions, with rhetors affirming or refuting the clam that an injustice had occurred. Examples of forensic rhetoric today still include the opening and closing statements made by prosecution and defence teams in a trial. But contemporary forensic rhetoric also encompasses research genres such as conference presentations, journal articles and book chapters, which seek to justify or refute knowledge claims of various kinds.

The third genre, **deliberative rhetoric**, deliberates the benefit or harmfulness of a future course of action. In Aristotle's time, deliberative rhetoric typically took place in the citizens' assembly, with the audience voting for or against the proposed action. But, deliberative rhetoric can also appear in didactic poems, sermons and other hortatory messages which exhort actions that bring benefit and dissuade from actions that bring harm. Obviously, what constitutes benefit and harm depends on the audience's core values. The more heterogeneous an audience (see section 3.5), the harder it is to find common ground about what exactly constitutes a benefit or a harm because of conflicting interests, priorities and needs.

4.3   Stasis theory as an invention resource

Within the five canons of rhetoric, **invention** refers to a method of selecting arguments appropriate to a specific genre of rhetoric and type of audience. As Karlyn Campbell and Susan Huxman observe, classical Greek and Roman rhetoricians understood that:

> ordinarily, rhetors do not create arguments from scratch, but rather appropriate and adapt arguments they discover in their research, in the course of their training, in reports of research by others, in other speeches or essays, in cultural ideas. These arguments are applied to new circumstances, and invention refers to the choice from among available argumentative options. Invention also reflects the creative role of the rhetor in selecting and adapting arguments and evidence in ways best suited to the occasion and audience and to his purpose, and in organizing these into an effective whole.

> (Campbell and Huxman, 2009, p.110)

Rhetoricians usually discuss invention in terms of Aristotle's **topoi**, or topics, and Quintilian's *stasis*. **Stasis** refers to a procedure of asking questions to determine the **point at issue** in an argument. If arguers don't clarify what exactly is at issue, they may end up arguing at cross-purposes (see *level of dispute* in section 1.2). **Stasis theory** involves asking four questions (see Figure 4.2).

Type of Stasis	Type of Question	Example questions
Conjectural	empirical truth	*Does X exist? Did X happen?*
Definitional	analytic truth	*What is X?*
Qualitative	value	*Is X good or bad?*
Procedural	policy	*Should we do X or not?*

Figure 4.2   The four questions of stasis theory

Conjectural stasis involves asking whether or not something is the case — whether a particular state of affairs exists, whether a particular chain of events occurred, what caused it and what its effects might be. In short, conjectural stasis engages questions of **empirical truth** relating to existence, origins and causality.

Definitional stasis also involves questions of truth, but a different kind of truth than empirical truth. As the label suggests, definitional stasis involves questions of definition, and definitions convey what philosophers label **analytic truth** — statements that are true by definition. Whereas empirical truth depends on empirical support (facts, artefacts, and interpretations of fact), analytic truth depends on the meanings assigned to words. Consider the two sentences below.

(a) *My uncle Samuel is a bachelor.*

(b) *A bachelor is an unmarried adult male.*

Sentence (a) is an empirical truth, whereas (b) is an analytic truth. To check the truth of (b), all we need do is consult one or more dictionaries to check whether the word *bachelor* means 'unmarried adult male'. In contrast, to verify the truth of (a), consulting a dictionary to ascertain the meaning of the word *bachelor* is just the first step because sentence (a) makes a 'factual' claim about uncle Samuel. To verify its truth, we need to check whether uncle Samuel has a spouse. If he does, sentence (a) will have been shown to be empirically false.

Both conjectural and definitional stasis focus on questions of truth. In contrast, **qualitative stasis** determines the point at issue in an argument by asking **questions of quality, or value**, judging whether something is good or bad, right or wrong, measured against a relevant (e.g. legal, moral, pragmatic aesthetic or scientific) standard. **Procedural stasis** in turn discovers the point at issue by asking **questions of policy** (what should or shouldn't be done).

The four questions of stasis theory form the basis of a **taxonomy of argument types** commonly used in argument textbooks (see Figure 4.3). Each stasis question leads to an answer, which functions as the main claim argued by the rhetor for the audience's acceptance. Combining stasis theory with speech act theory (see section 3.8), we can identify the type of speech act performed by each type of claim.

Type of Stasis	Argument Type	Claim	Speech act
Conjectural	Empirical	Truth (factual)	Representative
Definitional	Definitional	Truth (analytic)	Representative
Qualitative	Value	Value	Verdictive
Procedural	Policy	Policy	Directive

Figure 4.3   A taxonomy of argument types

4.4   Empirical arguments

As mentioned above, both empirical and definitional arguments engage questions of truth, the difference being the kind of truth (empirical or analytic) addressed by each. **Empirical arguments** answer empirical questions concerning existence (*Does X exist? Did X happen?*), origins (*Where did X come from?*) and causality (*What are the effects of X, and how are they produced?*), and depend on empirical support in the form of evidence comprising facts, artefacts and interpretation of facts. As suggested in section 1.2, 'facts' are assertions which lie below the *level of dispute* for a particular audience. The qualifier *for a particular audience* is important because facts can and do change, as new evidence comes in. So depending on our respective levels of knowledge about the issue being argued, what may be a 'fact' for you may not be a fact for me, and *vice versa*.

Activity 4.1

Which of the following statements is a fact?

1. Canberra is the capital of Australia.

2. Most people have ten fingers and ten toes.

3. Pluto is a dwarf planet.

4. Human males cannot give birth to children.

Comment on Activity 4.1

All four statements are facts, at this point in human history. Statements 2 and 4 are verifiable through observation, while statements 1 and 3 are matters of public record.

Empirical arguments are central to knowledge construction in personal, public and technical argument spheres (see section 2.8). Let's suppose we're arguing about whether or not a murder took place next door. The question at issue is an empirical one: Did a murder take place next door? To argue productively, we need to start by establishing **common ground**, identifying the self-evident truths, facts and assumptions that lie below the level of dispute (see Figure 1.4) for both of us, such as our shared assumption that something did occur next door. Second, we would need to establish a shared definition of *murder*. After all, there are at least four possible explanations for death: natural causes, suicide, accident and murder. And, what happened next door might perhaps be more accurately labelled *manslaughter* (unpremeditated homicide) rather than *murder* (premeditated homicide).

Similarly, a rhetor wishing to argue that Asian women are more feminine than western women would need to build common ground with the audience in terms of a shared **operational definition** of *femininity*, i.e. what exactly does the term entail so that it can be measured both validly and reliably, in practice? What both these examples illustrate is that all arguments begin with definition, but not all arguments are definitional arguments. So, that is the question we turn to next — defining definitional arguments.

4.5 Definitional arguments

Definitional arguments are so-named because they seek to define something. They ask *What is X?* and answer with the main claim *X is a Y* (e.g. *What is an Argument? An argument is a connected series of statements to establish a definite position*). The structure of the definitional claim *X is a Y* influences the rhetorical structure of definitional arguments, which comprise two rhetorical moves: **Defining Y** followed by **Criterion-matching**.

Let's start by considering **Move 1: Defining Y**. Broadly speaking, **definitions** specify two kinds of information organised in a *general-particular* pattern:

(1) the general class which **Y** is a member of, followed by

(2) the specific traits distinguishing **Y** from fellow members of the set.

Definitions display this textual pattern because concepts don't exist in splendid isolation but in networks. A word makes sense only in relation to words it is semantically related to such as its antonyms, synonyms, hyponyms and meronyms. For example, the word *boy* makes sense only in relation to beings that aren't boys, such as *girl* or *man*. To define *boy* in relation to *girl*, we could start with the general category *young human*, then use the variable SEX [-female] or [+male] to distinguish *boy* from *girl*. Similarly, to define *boy* in relation to *man*, we could begin with the class *male human*, then use the variable AGE [-adult] or [+child] to distinguish *boy* from *man*.

Dictionary definitions typically follow this *general-particular* text pattern. For example, if you look up the noun *drum*, you'll learn that *drum* falls within the general category of percussion instruments, before being given a description of a drum's form and function, which set it apart from fellow percussion instruments. Here's how the online *Oxford English Dictionary* defines *drum*:

> A musical instrument of the percussive class, consisting of a hollow cylindrical or hemispherical frame of wood or metal, with a 'head' of tightly stretched membrane at one or both ends, by the striking of which and the resonance of the cavity the sound is produced.
> (http://www.oed.com/view/Entry/58009?rskey=8I1Xua&result=1#eid)

You'll notice that we used a similar method to define *argument* in chapter 1, first highlighting argument as a subset of discourse, before defining its structure and purpose so as to distinguish it from discourse genres like *explanation* and *persuasion*.

Keep in mind that words have everyday meanings as well as more specialised technical meanings. Dictionaries typically codify the common meanings of words. For more specialised meanings, we need to consult technical dictionaries or discipline-specific manuals and handbooks. For example, if you wanted a legal definition of *obscenity*, you'd consult a Dictionary of Law; if you wanted a medical definition of *depression*, you'd look in a medical manual; and, if you were after a psychological definition of *neurosis*, you'd consult a handbook of psychology.

Further, given the multiple meanings that a word can have, arguers need to think carefully about which strategy to use (selection, synthesis or stipulation) when crafting definitions for the purposes of argument:

❖ **Selection** involves choosing the best definition from a list of alternatives.

❖ **Synthesis** involves weaving together different definitions.

❖ **Stipulation** involves stating a special meaning different from common meanings of a term.

Just as there is no 'one' correct way to do most things in life, there is no precise formula for building a good definition. Each method has its strengths and limitations, which rhetors must weigh carefully. All definitions (whether selected, synthesised or stipulated) work by foregrounding certain aspects of reality. When contemplating definitions (see Figure 4.4), ask yourself *Whose interests are served by this definition — who or what gets included/ excluded; who or what gets emphasised/marginalised?*

EXAMINING DEFINITIONS CRITICALLY

1. Does the rhetor **borrow** the definition — whose, and why? Does the rhetor's use of the definition accord with the definition's original purpose?

2. Does the rhetor provide **examples** to illustrate meaning — are the examples real or hypothetical, representative or atypical?

3. Does the definition invite **polarisation** (two mutually exclusive choices) by employing **complementary** rather than **gradable antonyms**?

4. What **tropes** and/or **schemes** (see chapter 6) does the rhetor use to amplify meaning?

Figure 4.4   Examining definitions critically

Activity 4.2

Which claim(s) below could trigger a definitional argument? Justify your answer!

1. *A foetus is not a person.*

2. *Depriving prisoners of sleep constitutes torture.*

3. *Education is a form of propaganda.*

Once an arguer has selected, synthesised or stipulated a clear, concise and coherent definition of **Y**, the second rhetorical move (***criterion-matching***) in a definitional argument involves mapping the criteria used to define **Y** onto X so as to demonstrate that **X** fulfils or matches these criteria.

4.6   Value arguments

Value arguments address the value-based question *Is X good or bad?* with *good* and *bad* being measured against some standard (legal, moral, pragmatic, aesthetic, scientific, etc.). Since value arguments argue the value of something, the main claim will feature evaluative language, conveying approbation or disapprobation, as illustrated below:

>   *Cheating is **morally reprehensible**.*

>   *Professor Bhattacharya is an **outstanding** educator.*

>   *It's **foolish** to spend more on defence than on education.*

Mills (2000) advises rhetors facing mixed audiences to address the priorities of hostiles, friendlies and neutrals (see section 3.5) sequentially. If this is not feasible, Mills (2000) counsels rhetors to direct their arguments to the powerful decision-makers in the audience.

But, even this can be tricky, since power can come from different sources, including legal power, celebrity power and 'people' power (strength in numbers).

When discussing values, it's important to keep in mind that people hold some values more deeply and fervently than others. These **core values**, as argument researchers Rieke and Sillars (2001) dub them, are the values least open to negotiation because they form the foundation of a person's identity. Social psychologist Milton Rokeach (1968) suggests that although people hold many different attitudes and beliefs, their core values probably only number a dozen or so.

Rokeach (1973) created a taxonomy of values comprising terminal and instrumental values by instructing survey participants to arrange each set of values "in their order of importance to YOU, as guiding principles in YOUR life" (p. 27). **Terminal values** refer to desirable end-states that a person would like to achieve while **instrumental values** refer to modes of behaviour that people engage in to achieve their terminal values.

Terminal Values (listed alphabetically)	
1. A comfortable life	10. Inner harmony
2. An exciting life	11. Mature love
3. A sense of accomplishment	12. National security
4. A world at peace	13. Pleasure
5. A world of beauty	14. Salvation
6. Equality	15. Self-respect
7. Family security	16. Social recognition
8. Freedom	17. True friendship
9. Happiness	18. Wisdom

Figure 4.5   Rokeach's (1973) terminal values

Instrumental Values (listed alphabetically)	
1. Ambition	10. Imagination
2. Broad-mindedness	11. Independence
3. Capability	12. Intellect
4. Cheerfulness	13. Logic
5. Cleanliness	14. Love
6. Courage	15. Obedience
7. Forgiveness	16. Politeness
8. Helpfulness	17. Responsibility
9. Hones	18. Self-Control

Figure 4.6   Rokeach's (1973) instrumental values

Rieke and Sillars (2001) in turn analyse values in terms of whether they're positive or negative, abstract or concrete, stated or implied. As they point out, our definition of a value as 'a conception of the desirable' puts a clearly positive cast on value concepts. However, for every positive concept there is at least one antithesis. So a statement of value can be either positive or negative. Earning opposes stealing, freedom opposes restraint, thrift opposes waste, knowledge opposes ignorance, pleasure opposes pain. Depending upon the strategy devised, if you argue against a specific proposal, you may do so by identifying positive values that oppose it or negative values that you associate with it.

(Rieke and Sillars, 2001, p.197)

The enlightenment value system underlying contemporary western thought, for example, reflects the following values:

POSITIVE: freedom, science, nature, rationality, democracy, fact, liberty, individualism, knowledge, intelligence, reason, natural rights, natural laws, progress, information

NEGATIVE: ignorance, superstition, inattention, thoughtlessness, error, indecision, irrationality, dictatorship, bookburning, falsehood, regression

(Rieke and Sillars, 2001, p.201)

Second, values are ideas and therefore abstract. So, we sometimes treat particular people, places and objects (the flag, the family, the Bible, the Star of David, etc.) as **concrete values** (Perelman & Olbrechts-Tyteca 1979, cited in Rieke and Sillars, 2001, p.197) working in tandem with abstract values:

For instance, to use authority figures as support is to use concrete values. However, you don't say to a friend, "I believe we should study harder because my father says so." You are more likely to argue, "We should study harder. My father says it will lead to greater success." The abstract value of "success" is linked to the concrete value of "father".

(Rieke and Sillars, 2001, p. 199)

Third, values can be stated or implied, as illustrated below:

Equality
STATED: *Equal* pay for *equal* work
IMPLIED: Women deserve the same pay as men for the same work.

Science
STATED: DNA research is a *scientific* triumph
IMPLIED: DNA research is virtually unquestionable.

Self-respect
STATED: Every child's well-being is based on *self-respect*.
IMPLIED: Children need to learn to like themselves.

(Rieke & Sillars, 2001, p.196-7)

Are you wondering how rhetors decide which values to state, where and when in their texts? Rieke and Sillars (2001) suggest that genre norms are a crucial consideration. For example, within the legal sphere, closing arguments are usually more **value explicit** than the witness-examination phase of the trial because of a shared norm that evidence collection ought to be as value-free as possible. So, a witness might say during questioning, "I saw the defendant take the money from the cash register and run from the store" (p.197), where the negative value of stealing is only implied. In contrast, during closing arguments, lawyers have greater freedom to openly attach values to the evidence as they sum up their respective cases. This observation certainly makes sense, given the primacy-recency effect discussed in section 3.6. Figure 4.7 summarises Rieke and Sillars' (2001, p.207) heuristic for examining value systems in arguments.

EXAMINING VALUES IN ARGUMENTS

1. What *proportion* of a value system is represented by negative or positive values, abstract or concrete values, terminal or instrumental values, stated or implied values?

2. What *emphasis* does the value system have? How value intensive is it? What values are most salient?

3. How *consistent* are the values within the system?

4. How *significant* are the values in the system to the decision-makers?

Figure 4.7   Examining values in arguments (Rieke and Sillars, 2001, p.207)

Activity 4.3

Write a clear, concise and coherent 500-word analysis, examining how horror fiction writer Stephen King employs values to argue his case in the essay 'Why we crave horror movies' (http://drmarkwomack.com/pdfs/horrormovies.pdf).

Activity 4.4

Select an argument, and write a clear, concise and coherent 500-word analysis, examining whether the opening and closing segments are more value explicit, as Rieke and Sillars (2001) suggest.

4.7 Policy arguments

Policy arguments form the mainstay of deliberative rhetoric, and result from the stasis question *Should we do X?* Policy arguments seek to exhort or dissuade an audience from a specific course of action, based on notions of benefit and harm. Those in favour of doing X argue *We should do X because doing X is more beneficial than doing Y (which may include doing nothing)* while those against doing X will argue *We should NOT do X because doing X would be more harmful than doing Y (which may include doing nothing).*

A policy is a systematic response to a particular situation. Unlike truth and value arguments, which seek to influence the audience's beliefs and attitudes, policy arguments seek to influence behaviour. And, we know how hard it can be to overcome human inertia (our penchant for procrastination). In addition, implementing a policy often requires the cooperation of diverse groups with competing agendas. All policy arguments thus have to address five **stock issues** (see Figure 4.8) in the form of a two-part **Problem-Solution** pattern.

Stock issue	Questions to consider
HARM	*Is there a compelling need to change the current policy — who's being harmed, and how?*
SIGNIFICANCE	*Is the harm significant enough to warrant action — how far-reaching and how great is the harm?*
INHERENCY	*Is the harm inherent to the policy — exactly how does the current policy generate harm?*
SOLUTION	*What's the solution, and exactly how will it solve the problem identified?*
ADVANTAGES	*In what way(s) is the proposed policy more beneficial than the current policy?*

Figure 4.8   The *stock issues* approach to policy argument

A **problem** is an aspect of a situation which requires a response because of the harm it's causing. The first three stock issues (harm, significance, inherency) frame the problem that the policy advocate is seeking to solve. As rhetors attempt to establish common ground (see section 1.4), they must ask two questions about the *problem*:

❖ ***Do they know?*** Does the audience share my view that this is a *problem* or do I need to show them why it's a problem?

❖ ***Do they care?*** Does the audience care enough about the problem to do something about it or do I need to demonstrate what's at stake?

Policy arguments are difficult because change is risky, and we tend to be risk-averse when we don't know whether the change will benefit us or whether the benefit will be worth the cost of change. So, **the burden of proof** falls on policy proponents to demonstrate that:

❖ someone is being harmed (stock issue 1);

❖ the harm is sufficiently significant to warrant action (stock issue 2); and,

❖ the harm is inherent to the current policy (stock issue 3).

The assertion that *someone is being harmed* involves questions of truth, definition and value, since *harm* is a value-laden concept, and what constitutes harm will vary from one context to another, as illustrated by rhetorical analysts Karlyn Campbell and Susan Huxman:

> Consider, for example, the startling fact that over 440,000 people in the United States die each year from the effects of smoking, a figure that dwarfs the 3,800-plus Americans killed since 2003 in the Iraq War. Those deaths have generated national debate over setting a date for the removal of US troops. The deaths from smoking have been an accepted part of our culture for many years, and until quite recently little had been done to reduce those numbers. As these examples illustrate, a claim that some situation is harmful combines data with a justification drawn from a value.
>
> (Campbell & Huxman, 2009, p.108)

Most arguers demonstrate significant harm, using **statistics** displaying the breadth (wide reach) and depth (level or magnitude) of the harm. In situations where statistics are unavailable and where lives are at stake, a single **telling example** may suffice to raise the alarm. For instance, in the 2011 Fukushima nuclear meltdown in Japan, the release of substantial amounts of radioactive material into the air, food and water supply called into question the policy of allowing the construction of nuclear power plants in earthquake-prone zones. Similarly, a single catastrophic event like 9/11 has led to the tightening of security at airports and border checkpoints not just in America but around the globe.

A third way to demonstrate significant harm is to *change the frame to change the game*, as ad man Rory Sutherland (2009) recommends. This is exactly what a student advocating universal mandatory measles vaccinations did to transform the topic

> from triviality to significance by citing evidence to show how many unvaccinated children would get the measles, how many of those children would be permanently brain damaged, and what would be the cost to society. Suddenly, a rather unimportant, previously remote childhood disease became a significant social problem with important financial implications for each of us.
>
> (Campbell & Huxman, 2009, p.108)

Legal advocate Bryan Stevenson, similarly, shifts the focus from criminals to us, in this excerpt from his *Ted2012* talk 'We need to talk about an injustice' (which can be viewed on YouTube and at www.ted.com):

> I represent people on death row. It's interesting, this question of the death penalty. In many ways, we've been taught to think that the real question is: Do people

deserve to die for the crimes they've committed? And that's a very sensible question. But there's another way of thinking about where we are in our identity. The other way of thinking about it is not do people deserve to die for the crimes they commit, but do we deserve to kill?

Once a rhetor has demonstrated that harm exists and that it is significant, the third stock issue (inherency) requires rhetors to demonstrate that the significant harm they've identified is inherent to the current policy, explaining exactly how the current policy generates significant harm as its inevitable result.

Once the problem has been framed in terms of harm, significance and inherency, the stage is set for the rhetor to introduce his/her policy recommendation. As the audience weighs the merits of the proposed policy, they will be wondering if the policy is meant to:

❖ prevent or cure the harm

❖ treat the symptoms or eradicate the root cause

❖ reverse the problem or merely prevent it from getting worse

❖ solve the whole problem or only some part(s)

So, wise rhetors will anticipate these questions, explaining how exactly their policy will work. And, since there's usually more than one way to solve a problem, they will need to demonstrate not only that their solution will work but that it represents the best available solution. The final two stock issues (solution, advantages) relate to the feasibility and the superiority respectively of the policy being advocated.

Aristotle suggests that the central issue of deliberative rhetoric is appropriateness to the purpose at hand, i.e. the proposed action must be perceived by the audience as the most effective and efficient means to the desired end. In weighing the merits of the proposed policy, the audience will basically engage in cost-benefit analysis, judging the available solutions to determine which best fits their core values (see section 4.5), in terms of simplicity, convenience, safety, etc., all else being equal. Audiences will also likely speculate about the side-effects and unintended consequences of the proposed policy. Once again, trustworthy rhetors will anticipate these concerns to make it easier for the audience to weigh the merit of the proposed policy.

Activity 4.5

Working with a group of friends, form two teams to debate the policy question *Should students cheat on exams?* You can use the *stock issues* as an invention heuristic. Or, you can work intuitively, then look to see which of the stock issues you've addressed in your argument.

4.8   Aristotle's topics as an invention resource

Like Stasis Theory, Aristotle's **topoi** (topics) represent locations for discovering possible and permissible means of persuasion. For Aristotle, the tasks of the orator are "to find aspects of the subject that can be employed in arguments designed to establish the features that need to be stressed and that can be used to induce the appropriate emotional state in the listener and to create the appropriate impression of [the arguer's] character" (Lawson-Tancred, 1991, p.17). (NB: Did you spot the allusion to Aristotle's rhetorical appeals of *logos, pathos* and *ethos* in that quotation?) Aristotle identified two types of *topoi* (singular: *topos*):

❖ **common topics** (universal lines of argument applicable to all fields) and

❖ **special topics** (field-dependent arguments emerging out of specific disciplines, like law, medicine, economics and so on).

Scott Crider (2005, pp.29-30) translates Aristotle's common topics into five questions which rhetors can employ to invent arguments (see Figure 4.9).

Topics	Questions derived from the Common Topics
Definition	*Can I define X?* What are its general and specific characteristics?
Comparison	*Can I compare X and Y?* To what degree are they alike?
Relationship	*What's the relationship between X and Y?* Is it cause and effect, antecedent and consequence, contraries or contradictions?
Circumstance	*What are the circumstances of X?* Are they impossible, possible, improbable, probable or certain?
Testimony	*What support is there for X?* arguments from authority, witness statements, statistics, maxims, laws and/or precedents

Figure 4.9   Aristotle's common topics

The overlap between stasis theory and Aristotle's topics should be apparent. It should also be fairly obvious why the first topic or question tends to be definition, given that knowledge-construction begins with categorisation. For example, when 9/11 happened, someone had to define what happened. And, definitions, as we now know, involve pattern-matching, paying close attention to similarities and differences. Thus, there were comparisons between the 9/11 attack and the 1941 attack on Pearl Harbour.

Further, when something happens, we ask ourselves, has this happened before, when, where, how and why? For example, when the subprime market meltdown occurred in 2008, lots of people wondered whether we were headed for another depression like the Great Depression of the 1930s. To answer that question, economists and investors intuitively used the topics of **Comparison, Relationship** and **Circumstance**, looking for causes and effects in light of past certainties (facts) and future possibilities, while citing **Testimony** of various kinds including statistical data, economic theory, and the judgments of respected authorities.

Activity 4.6

What purpose does the comparison in the excerpt below serve? Justify your answer clearly, concisely and coherently.

Technology, like gambling and heroin, is addictive. We're driven or forced into buying new gadgets and constantly upgrading our technology for any number of reasons, both real and perceived, and feel uncomfortable without our latest "fix". Corporations love this because once we accept and begin using their products or services, the dependency is formed and they essentially own our information and, subsequently society and us.

But unlike many other industries from the Industrial Age and the heroin dealers, high-tech corporations are in a unique position to determine – and force – us addicts to spend money, while relinquishing our rights to seek recourse for damages arising from their faulty products no matter what pain we must endure during our period of indentured servitude and addiction to their problematic technologies. In some cases, particularly in mainstream operating systems, software, and internet-based services, it's one step short of blackmail. We all certainly can't go cold turkey very easily, although some may try and succeed.

Forno, Richard. High Tech Heroin, *Perspective magazine*, October 3, 2003
http://news.cnet.com/2010-7355-5084320.html

4.9 Aristotle's rhetorical appeals as an invention resource

Thus far, we've looked at stasis theory and Aristotle's topics as invention resources. Both these resources can be coupled with a third invention resource — Aristotle's rhetorical appeals of *ethos, pathos* and *logos* (see section 3.5). Argument teachers Ramage, Bean and Johnson (2010) emphasise that while it may be tempting to think of *logos, ethos* and *pathos* as ingredients that you add to a text, like spices to a dish, a more accurate analogy would comprise the different lamps and filters used on theatre spotlights to vary the lighting effects on stage:

> Thus, if you switch on a *pathos* lamp (possibly through using more concrete language or vivid examples), the resulting image will engage the audience's sympathy and emotions more deeply. If you overlay an *ethos* filter (perhaps by adopting a different tone toward your audience), the projected image of the writer as a person will be subtly altered. If you switch on a *logos* lamp (by adding, say, more data for evidence), you will draw the reader's attention to the logical appeal of the argument. Depending on how you modulate the lamps and filters, you shape and color your readers' perception of you and your argument.
>
> (Ramage, Bean, & Johnson, 2010, p.109)

Based on this analogy and the primacy-recency effect discussed in section 3.6, we could ask various research questions about how a rhetor modulates *logos, pathos* or *ethos* during a rhetorical performance. How, for example, is *ethos* performed in the opening as opposed to the end of an argument? If the rhetor relies heavily on *pathos* at the beginning and end of an argument, which values (terminal/instrumental; positive/negative; abstract/concrete — see section 4.6) does s/he appeal to in these segments, and how are they conveyed — implicitly or explicitly? Just as the lighting in a theatrical performance shifts and changes as a play unfolds, creating different moods and atmospheres, so also *logos, ethos* and *pathos* combine dynamically to create shifting moods in a rhetorical performance.

Aristotle's key contribution to the study of rhetoric was his awareness that compelling arguments employ appeals of reason, emotion and character simultaneously. In Book II of his *Rhetoric*, Aristotle discusses a whole gamut of emotions, which represent the outward expression of our core values (see section 4.5). For instance, if you feel pity for an abused child or feel anger over animal abuse, these emotions probably stem from a core value that sentient beings should not be ill-treated.

The psychologist Abraham Maslow (1943) famously depicted the hierarchy of human needs ranked in the order that people want satisfied (see Figure 4.10), from physiological needs at the base of the pyramid to self-actualisation at the top. Whether or not one accepts their hierarchical order, these needs and the values they embody can be a useful heuristic for rhetors and analysts alike.

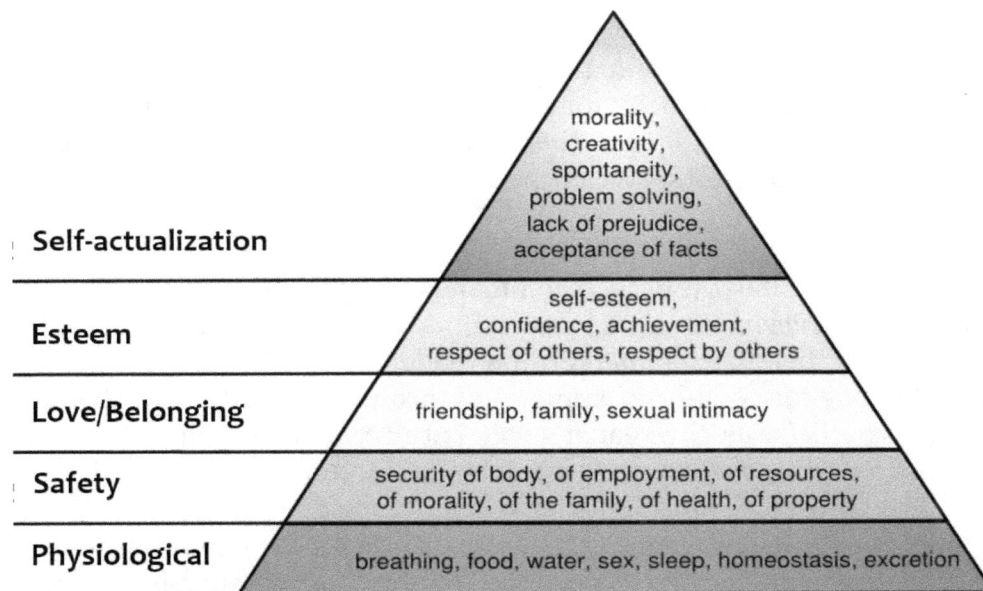

Figure 4.10   Maslow's (1943) hierarchy of needs

4.10 Rhetoric as the practice of critical assent

Most people think of rhetoric as a means of managing dissent. But, rhetorician Wayne Booth (2005) advocates focusing on rhetoric as the practice of critical assent, arguing that in the attempt to avoid blind faith, rhetoric may have swung too far in the opposite direction resulting in blind scepticism. According to Booth (2005), the goal of rhetoric as critical assent is "never to assent to or reject any new position...[we] have not fully understood" (p.386) because the right to criticise must be earned by "dwelling with" and "dwelling in" (Booth, 1979, cited in Elbow, 2005, p.389) a person's ideas.

Almost two decades earlier, psychotherapist Carl Rogers (1961) identified the sense of threat engendered by "our very natural tendency to judge, to evaluate, to approve or disapprove, the statement of the other person, or the other group" (p. 28) as a major barrier to communication:

> Real communication occurs, and this evaluative tendency is avoided, when we listen with understanding. What does this mean? It means to see the expressed idea and attitude from the other person's point of view, to sense how it feels to him, to achieve his frame of reference in regard to the thing he is talking about.
>
> (Rogers, 1961, p. 29)

Rogers dubs *listening with understanding* **empathic listening**, the core of what Edward Inch and Barbara Warnick (2010) label a "co-orientational approach to argument [which] presumes that the relationship between arguer and recipient is as important as the content of the argument" (p.34).

Inspired by Rogers' (1961) idea of empathic listening, Booth (2005) advocates a method of **active listening**, in which we speak up for our own view only after we have first restated or paraphrased our interlocutor's ideas to their satisfaction. In short, we need to listen well enough to our interlocutors, to serve as their advocate, even if we disagree with their position.

Writing professor Peter Elbow (2005) recommends a slightly different route to the same goal — playing the *believing/doubting game*, in which the reader alternates between extremes of doubt and belief. As a *doubter*, the reader's role is to be wholly skeptical of a writer's claims, looking for counter-examples and inconsistencies that weaken the writer's case. Conversely, as a *believer*, the reader's role is to try and see things from the writer's frame of reference, entering the writer's worldview no matter how alien it might feel.

One way to play the believing game is to write *says/does* summaries (Ramage, Bean & Johnson, 2010). *Says* statements summarise content. *Does* statements summarise the rhetorical actions performed by a writer in a segment of text, as illustrated below:

Paragraph 1   *introduces the problem of illegal prostitution with an anecdote*

Paragraph 2   *sketches two opposing views to legalised prostitution*

Paragraph 3   *refutes the first view using statistics*

The strategies of active listening, playing the believing/doubting game, and writing says/does summaries are three ways of discovering common ground with the audience. Unlike adversarial argument which adopts a win-lose zero-sum view of argument, non-adversarial argument acknowledges that two ideas that appear logically contradictory may both be viable if viewed from a larger perspective. This view of argument resonates with the philosophical position known as **Hegelian dialectic**. The 19th century German philosopher Hegel believed that human thought developed through three stages — believing an idea (thesis) then inevitably doubting it (antithesis) before arriving at a more holistic insight (synthesis).

Although the term dialectic has many definitions, Hegelian dialectic sees us moving beyond our initial *pro* or *con* ideas to a more richly nuanced and fuller understanding of things. Think, for example, about the 17th century controversy over the nature of light — is light a particle or a wave? The answer, we now know, is both. What this example illustrates is the danger of falling prey to binary or polarised thinking, what logic textbooks label the either-or fallacy or black-and-white thinking. Hegelian dialectic reminds us to beware **false dichotomies**, by considering more than two possibilities (*Yes, No, Maybe… Now, Never, Later…*).

Writing researcher Andrea Lunsford (1979) highlights how in Book II of the *Rhetoric*, Aristotle stresses the importance of "get[ting] the audience in the right frame of mind" (ii, 1, p.91) by evincing an *ethos* that is conciliatory, honest and understanding of the audience's needs and beliefs. Here is how rhetorician Kenneth Burke explains the same idea:

> You persuade a man only insofar as you can talk his language by speech, gesture, tonality, order, image, attitude, idea, — identifying your ways with his…. True, the rhetorician may have to change an audience's opinion in one respect; but he can succeed only insofar as he yields to that audience's opinions in other respects.
>
> (Burke, 1962, cited in Lunsford, 1979, p.150)

Doing *ethos* involves demonstrating respect for one's interlocutors even when one disagrees with them. As Maxine Hairston (1976) puts it, "you do not convert people to your point of view by threatening them or challenging their values" (p.373). Instead, the ethical rhetor seeks mutual trust, common ground to build bridges rather than walls between alternative viewpoints.

Activity 4.7

Which reading of Wordsworth's poem do you trust more, and why?

Wordsworth's poem
A slumber did my spirit seal;
    I had no human fears:
She seemed a thing that could not feel
    The touch of earthly years.
No motion had she now, no force,

She neither hears nor sees;
Rolled round in earth's diurnal course,
    With rocks, and stones, and trees.

Cleanth Brooks's (1951) analysis of the poem

[Wordsworth] attempts to suggest something of the lover's agonized shock at the loved one's present lack of motion—of his response to her utter and horrible inertness...He chooses to suggest it...by imagining her in violent motion....Part of the effect, of course, resides in the fact that a dead lifelessness is suggested more sharply by an object's being whirled around by something else than by an image of the object in repose. But there are other matters which are at work here: the sense of the girl's falling back into the clutter of things, companioned by things chained like a tree to one particular spot, or by things completely inanimate, like rocks and stones....She is touched by and held by earthly time in its most powerful and horrible image.

                Brooks, Cleanth. (1951) "Irony as a Principle of Structure", in M.D. Zabel (Ed.)
                                Literary Opinion in America (2nd edition) New York: Harper, p.736.

Monroe Beardsley's (1970) response to Brooks (1951)

Brooks's reading is (uncharacteristically) distorted. Lucy is not "whirled"; she is "rolled." She does not fall back into a "clutter of things", but is placed among trees, which do not really suggest "dead lifelessness." An orderly "diurnal course" is not "violent motion." Brooks has simply substituted words with connotations quite absent from the poem, and built his own "horrible image" out of them.

....

The words "rocks" and "stones" and "trees" are placed in parallel syntactic positions, which suggests that the objects that they denote are similar in some important respect. But a suggestion that two different things are similar can go in either direction, and we have to decide between them. We could take the parallelism as suggesting that the trees (and a fortiori the dead Lucy) are like rocks and stones, blind passive victims of external mechanical forces. But one could take the comparison the other way and come out with the opposing interpretation: by putting the word "trees" at the end, the speaker gives it emphasis; therefore he is really suggesting that rocks and stones (and a fortiori the dead Lucy) are like trees in having an inner life of their own.

Thus, we can bring the issue to a fairly sharp decision point. If the speaker is suggesting that Lucy and trees are like rocks and stones, we have a hint of mechanistic materialism. If he is suggesting that rocks and stones and Lucy are like trees, then we have a hint of pantheism (or at least animism)

Consider next a connotation problem. The speaker says that the dead Lucy has no force, no motion, and no sense-awareness – but then he says that she does have a motion, after all, since she lies near the surface of the earth and thus participates fully in its rotation. She is "rolled round in earth's diurnal course." The question is how much can we legitimately find in the meaning of "rolled" here? Now the available repertoire of connotations for the word "rolled" is certainly quite rich....But what about the present context? Here what must strike us forcible is the way the other words in this line qualify and specify the motion that Lucy has: it is a regular motion, with a constant rate; it is a comparatively slow and gently motion, since one revolution takes twenty-four hours; it is an orderly motion, since it follows a simple circular path.

In none of these aspects is it terrifying or demeaning; if anything, it is comforting and elevating. If we accept these connotations, the poem contains a hint of pantheism, or at least animism.

Beardsley, Monroe C. (1970) *The Possibility of Criticism.*
Detroit: Wayne State University, pp. 29, 45-47.

Having explored how rhetors invent arguments in response to questions of truth, value and policy, using heuristic devices like stasis theory, the stock issues of policy argument, Aristotle's topics and rhetorical appeals (*logos, ethos, pathos*), we turn in the next chapter to the issues that rhetors consider, when deciding how to organise their arguments in the best possible order for the audience and rhetorical purpose at hand.

References

Aristotle. *The Art of Rhetoric.* (1991). Translated with an introduction and notes by Hugo Lawson-Tancred. Harmondsworth: Penguin Classics.

Booth, Wayne C. (2005). Blind skepticism versus a rhetoric of assent. *College English, 67*(4), 378–388.

Campbell, Karlyn K. and Huxman, Susan S. (2009). *The Rhetorical Act: Thinking, speaking and writing critically* (4th edition). Belmont, CA: Wadsworth Cengage Learning.

Clifton, Jonathan and van de Mieroop, Dorien. (2010). 'Doing' ethos—A discursive approach to the strategic deployment and negotiation of identities in meetings. *Journal of Pragmatics 42*, 2449-2461.

Elbow, Peter. (2005). Bringing the rhetoric of assent and the believing game together—and into the classroom. *College English, 67*(4), 388–399.

Hairston, Maxine. (1976) Carl Rogers's Alternative to Traditional Rhetoric. *College Composition and Communication 27(4)*, 373-377.

Inch, Edward S. and Warnick, Barbara (2010). *Critical Thinking And Communication: The use of reason in argument* (6th edition). Boston: Allyn & Bacon.

Lawson-Tancred, Hugo. (Trans.). (1991). *The Art of Rhetoric.* Harmondsworth: Penguin Classics, pp.1-58.

Lunsford, Andrea. (1979). Aristotelian vs. Rogerian Argument: A Reassessment. *College Composition and Communication 30(2)*, pp.146-151.

Maslow, Abraham. (1943). A theory of human motivation. *Psychological Review 50(4),* pp. 370-96.

Mills, Harry. (2000). *Artful Persuasion: How to command attention, change minds, and influence people.* New York: AMACOM.

Ramage, John, Bean, John and Johnson, June. (2010). *Writing arguments: A rhetoric with readings* (8th ed.). New York: Longman.

Rieke, Richard D. and Sillars, Malcolm O. (2001). *Argumentation and Critical Decision Making* (5th ed.) New York: Longman.

Rogers, Carl. (1961). Communication: Its blocking and its facilitation. *On becoming a person* (pp. 27–34). New York: Houghton.

Rokeach, Milton. (1968). *Beliefs, Attitudes, and Values.* San Francisco: Jossey-Bass.

Rokeach, Milton. (1973). *The Nature of Human Values.* San Francisco: Free Press.

Sutherland, Rory (2009). Life Lessons from an Ad Man. Ted Talk. Retrieved June 14, 2011, from http://www.ted.com/talks/lang/eng/rory_sutherland_life_lessons_from_an_ad_man.html

Chapter 5 Organisation

How and where do I start?

Should I include opposing views?

Should I include all my arguments, even weak ones?

Where should I place my strongest argument?

5.1   How and where do I start?

The canon of invention helps rhetors select the rhetorical appeals (*logos, pathos, ethos*) best suited to audience (friendlies, neutrals, hostiles), rhetorical purpose (forensic, epideictic, deliberative) and argument issue (truth, value, policy). The canon of organisation in turn helps rhetors sequence this material. **Classical organisation** comprised five parts, as shown in Figure 5.1.

BEGINNING	**Part 1: Introduction** (*exordium*)	leads the audience into the argument, providing needed background to frame and focus the issue
	Part 2: Outline (*narration*)	provides a road-map forecasting the argument's overall shape
MIDDLE	**Part 3: the proof** (*confirmation*)	develops support for the argument
	Part 4: the refutation (*refutation*)	responds to objections
END	**Part 5: the conclusion** (*peroration*)	returns the audience to the real-world

Figure 5.1   **The five elements of classical organisation**

Beginnings and endings represent prime locations in a text, given the primacy-recency effect highlighted in section 3.6. Beginnings and endings are also notoriously difficult because rhetors have to decide how far back to begin and how far forward to end. In terms of **rhetorical structure**, the opening of an argument performs two rhetorical moves: introducing the rhetor's purpose and outlining the argument.

The introduction leads the audience into the text, anticipating and responding to the audience's question *Why should I pay attention to you?* The rhetor's task in this section is to frame and focus the issue so that it's clear to the audience why the rhetor's argument is worth attending to. How the rhetor does this will depend on the issue being argued, what the audience already knows and feels about the issue and the rhetor (see section 3.5) as well as the communicative norms of the genre being employed. For example, while it may be appropriate to make small talk or share personal anecdotes in the preamble to face-to-face negotiations, the same behaviour would represent a marked choice in written genres like the research article, where the expectation is for arguers to get straight to business.

The primary purpose of research articles is to convince a jury of one's peers to accept the knowledge claim being proposed, moving it from the level of conjecture to the level of 'fact' (Latour and Woolgar, 1986). In his book-length study of research articles (RAs), applied linguist John Swales (1990) shows how RA writers create a research space in their introductions by performing three consecutive rhetorical moves: identifying the research area, establishing a niche within this area, and occupying this niche.

In performing these three moves, RA introductions exhibit a general-particular discourse pattern, as writers map out the research terrain before specifying the issue, question or problem that their study addresses. The first move (identifying the research area) is akin to the establishing shot in a movie, while the second and third moves (establishing and occupying the niche, respectively) tighten the frame to a medium then close-up shot. Swales (1990, p.141) dubs this rhetorical-move structure the *Create a Research Space* (CARS) model, and outlines four alternative ways in which a writer can perform *Move 2 Establishing a niche* (counter-claiming, indicating a gap in the existing research, question-raising or continuing a research tradition).

Almost two hundred years earlier, 19th century rhetorician Richard Whately (1828, cited by Crider, 2005:50-52) offered the following five possibilities for opening an argument:

Introduction type	What it does
Inquisitive	leads readers into the text by posing a question to explore
Paradoxical	leads readers into the text by persuading them that although the case seems improbable, it is true
Corrective	persuades readers that the issue has not been addressed adequately, and that the rhetor will correct this situation
Preparatory	persuades readers that some unusual feature of the case is worth attending to
Narrative	persuades readers by narrating details leading to the case at hand

Figure 5.2   Whately's opening gambits

University educators Phyllis Creme and Mary Lea (2008) emphasise that it is difficult to lay down rules as to what exactly introductions should look like, while offering a list of things that argument introductions usually do:

- ❖ provide an overview of what the piece will be about
- ❖ present the central idea of the piece
- ❖ explain the motivation for writing this piece
- ❖ explain how the issue will be addressed
- ❖ give reasons for addressing the issue in a particular way
- ❖ introduce the questions the piece will be addressing
- ❖ give the background/history/context to the issue addressed in the piece
- ❖ make a bold statement that the text will amplify and justify
- ❖ quote someone in order to interest the reader and give a feel of what the text is about
- ❖ present a concrete example or story which the piece will explain or elaborate upon
- ❖ relate the topic to other work in the same field
- ❖ convey the writer's own relationship to the material and to the reader, and a sense of their own voice in the assignment.

Overall, Creme and Lea (2008) suggest, the major function of the introduction is "to provide the reader with a clear signpost to where the whole piece is going" (p.144). Based on Whately's (1828), Swales's (1990) and Creme and Lea's (2008) work, we can infer that argument introductions typically perform three rhetorical moves:

(1) attracting the audience's attention (because persuasion requires the audience to stop and listen to, read or view the rhetor's message);

(2) previewing the arguer's argument (providing the audience with a road-map of the argument's global structure to aid comprehension and recall); and

(3) whetting the audience's appetite for more (if the introduction fails to generate sufficient interest, they may stop paying attention).

Activity 5.1

Which of Whately's opening gambits do you see below? Explain your reasoning clearly, concisely and coherently.

Excerpt 1

A few short years ago, I lay at the point of death. A congestive heart failure was treated for diagnostic purposes by an angiogram that triggered a stroke. Violent and painful hiccups, uninterrupted for several days and nights, prevented the ingestion of food. My left side and one of my vocal cords became paralyzed. Some form of pleurisy set in, and I felt I was drowning in a sea of slime. At one point, my heart stopped beating; just as I lost consciousness, it was thumped back into action again. In one of my lucid intervals during those days of agony, I asked my physician to discontinue all life-supporting services or show me how to do it. He refused and predicted that someday I would appreciate the unwisdom of my request.

A month later, I was discharged from the hospital. In six months, I regained the use of my limbs, and although my voice still lacks its old resonance and carrying power, I no longer croak like a frog. There remain some minor disabilities and I am restricted to a rigorous, low-sodium diet. I have resumed my writing and research.

Hook, Sidney (1978). In Defense of Voluntary Euthanasia, *The New York Times*, January 10, 1978.

Excerpt 2

We are in Seattle arguing for a world trade system that puts basic human rights and the environment at its core. We have the most powerful corporations of the world ranged against us. They own the media that informs us - or fails to inform us. And they probably own the politicians too. It's enough to make anybody feel a little edgy.

So here's a question for the world trade negotiators. Who is the system you are lavishing so much attention on supposed to serve?

We can ask the same question of the gleaming towers of Wall Street or the City of London - and the powerful men and women who tinker with the money system which drives world trade. Who is this system for?

Trading With Principles. Speech given by Anita Roddick at International Forum on Globalisation's Tech-In. Seattle, Washington. November 27, 1999
http://www.famousquotes.me.uk/speeches/Anita%20Roddick/index.htm

Excerpt 3

Dostoevsky once wrote that "in the end they will lay their freedom at our feet and say to us, 'Make us your slaves, but feed us.'" His prophecy is relevant when examining the modern information age—a dark, corporate-controlled society predicted by such artistic legends as Bruce Sterling, George Lucas, Ridley Scott and William Gibson.

We want to be part of this information environment and feel more empowered with each new gadget, service or digital connection in our lives. From packets to pagers, wireless to wired, the sun never sets in the information age; we are always plugged into the global matrix of the information domain. We're addicted to it and constantly awash in a sea of electronic stimuli.

Yet as we rush to embrace the latest and greatest gadgetry or high-tech service and satisfy our techno-craving, we become further dependent on these products and their manufacturers—so dependent that when something breaks, crashes, or is attacked, our ability to function is reduced or eliminated. Given these frequent technical and legal problems, I'm wondering if we're as free and empowered as we've been led to believe.

Forno, Richard. High Tech Heroin, *Perspective magazine*, October 3, 2003
http://news.cnet.com/2010-7355-5084320.html

5.2   Should I state my claim or imply it?

In section 3.9, we saw how addressers sometimes use indirect speech acts to imply their meaning. When organising an argument, rhetors must consider HOW best to convey their main claim (explicitly or implicitly) and WHEN and WHERE to articulate it (at the beginning or towards the end of the text). Persuasion researcher Stewart Tubbs considers the relative merits of explicit versus implicit claims highlighting the following paradox:

> One of the most striking implications of recent research in persuasion is that persuasive speeches designed to directly confront and convert an audience are, by and large, doomed to failure. In fact, the greater the discrepancy between the belief of an audience and the position supported by the speaker, the smaller will be the resulting attitude change. This is the conclusion arrived at by Berelson and Steiner in their review and research on attitude change.
>
> Based on research findings such those described above, the following conclusions seem supportable: (1) strong prior attitudes will render audiences receptive to congenial communications and resistant to uncongenial; (2) communications are most likely to persuade those in the audience who are neutral on an issue and least likely to persuade those who are highly committed on the issue.
>
> (Tubbs, 1968, p.14)

Citing Tubbs's (1968) study, Inch and Warnick (2010) highlight the advantages and disadvantages of stating one's claim, observing that some audiences may consider an explicit claim indicative of propaganda, while others may view an implicit claim as the sign of an incomplete argument. What Tubbs (1968) found was that "regardless of the audience's degree of commitment, the explicit conclusion was more effective in eliciting attitude change" (p.17) because "when claims are not explicitly stated, audiences fill in the gaps with claims and arguments of their own — ones that frequently go against what the arguer had intended" (Inch and Warnick, 2010, p.197). In other words, left to their own devices, audiences may misconstrue an arguer's intentions (see the gap between purpose and outcome, discussed in section 3.8).

It's worth pausing at this point to consider **cultural preferences**. Research in contrastive rhetoric (see Kaplan, 1966 and Connor, 1996) suggests that different cultures show distinct preferences both for rhetorical organisation and the proportion of explicit to implicit information in an argument. Linguist John Hinds (1983), for instance, notes how East Asian languages generally tend to be *reader-responsible*, unlike western rhetoric, which tends to be *writer-responsible*. In western rhetoric, the onus is on the writer to be maximally clear, and if communication breaks down, the blame tends to be placed on the writer for not being direct enough.

In contrast, eastern rhetoric shows a greater tolerance for implicit communication, given the politeness norm that imposing one's claim on others threatens their negative face. The assumption here is that readers (and listeners) are perceptive enough to connect the dots to reach the conclusion desired by the rhetor. And, certainly, even in the west, if a speech is extremely well organised, intelligent audiences may consider an explicitly-stated claim an insult to their intelligence.

When it comes to unsolicited texts, however, western rhetoric tends to favour explicit messages that get straight to the point in terms of informing audiences why it's in their best interests to pay attention to the text at hand. Academic audiences typically fall into this group, as do other busy decision-makers in the technical argument sphere.

In contrast, there are two competing pulls in the public argument sphere. For unsolicited texts, western audiences generally prefer getting straight down to business. So, it makes sense to state the argument claim as early and clearly as possible to pre-empt the audience misconstruing the arguer's intent.

What happens, however, if the claim happens to be about a hot-button issue where emotions are running high, such as in value and policy arguments seeking to change deeply and fervently held attitudes and behaviours? Let's suppose a rhetor wishes to persuade an audience of young adults to stop smoking. If s/he begins by stating the claim *You should stop smoking* upfront, the audience may immediately throw up its deflector shields, refusing to listen further.

In such situations, rhetors have the same problem as sales people whose advances we seek to avoid. To get their foot in the door, these sales folk camouflage their true intent. The same phenomenon can be observed in hybrid genres like *advertorials* (advertisements disguised as editorials) and *infommercials* (commercials pretending to be purveyors of information rather than products). The demands of ethical persuasion (see section 3.6) require rhetors not to engage in such subterfuge, as a hostile audience may perceive such behaviour as deceptive and manipulative.

So, how can rhetors get their foot in the door, ethically? One way is to delay stating one's claim. In **classical arguments**, the claim is presented first followed by the basis for the claim (*Claim > Basis for Claim*). In **delayed-claim arguments**, this sequence is reversed (*Basis for Claim > Claim*). The idea is that as the audience accepts each point marshalled in support of the rhetor's overall claim, they will connect the dots so as to arrive at the conclusion desired by the rhetor.

Some argument textbooks refer to these two kinds of organisation as deductive (*Claim > Basis*) and inductive (*Basis > Claim*). But, I prefer reserving the labels *deductive* and *inductive* for two common patterns of reasoning. **Inductive reasoning** entails reasoning from particular to general cases, and is common to both statistical sample and anecdotal reasoning (e.g. *Most of the Martians on this spaceship are green. So, in the absence of evidence to the contrary, it's reasonable to conclude that Martians are green.*). In contrast, **deductive reasoning** involves reasoning either from general to particular cases or from cause to effect, as illustrated in Figure 5.3.

Examples of deductive reasoning	
GENERAL-TO-PARTICULAR	**CAUSE-TO-EFFECT**
All neeblies are gleeks.	*Sleep deprivation causes tiredness.*
Joel is a neebly.	*Sarah is sleep deprived.*
Therefore, Joel is a gleek.	*Therefore, Sarah will be tired.*

Figure 5.3   Examples of deductive reasoning

Whichever organisation (classical or delayed claim) one selects, it's worth following psychotherapist Carl Rogers' (1961) advice to practice **empathic listening** throughout, especially when addressing hostile audiences (see section 3.5 and Figure 5.5). Echoing Rogers's recommendation, Inch and Warnick (2010) emphasise that "[t]he single most important skill an arguer must master is the art of listening carefully to what others say—both in preparation and in presentation of arguments" (p.196). Inch and Warnick distinguish three kinds of listening: active, passive and competitive.

> *Active listening means to hear for meaning.* Arguers should listen to *how* something is said as much as to *what* is said. They should endeavor to understand the meaning of the message as the speaker intended it. Active listening is different from other types of listening. It is not an easy skill to master and involves careful concentration and reflective questions, but it is important.
>
> (Inch and Warnick, 2010, p.196)

Writing *says/does* summaries and playing the *believing/doubting* game (see section 4.10) are two strategies that can help with **active listening**.

Passive listening, meanwhile, "*involves hearing other points of view without verifying or affirming understanding*" (Inch and Warnick, 2010, p.196, italics in original). Rhetors who listen passively hear arguments and respond to what they heard, presuming that they've correctly understood the speaker or writer's intent without actually taking the trouble to verify whether their interpretation is in fact accurate — a dangerous thing to do, given that most people tend to overestimate their ability to decode others' intentions.

Competitive listening in turn

> *is characterised by advocates who are more interested in winning an argument or a particular position rather than understanding other viewpoints.* Academic debate, legislative assemblies, and political debates are all contexts in which competitive listening can dominate.
>
> (Inch and Warnick, 2010, p.196, italics in original)

As emphasised throughout this volume, the goal of argument is not to score points off one another but to *win* an audience *over* to the rhetor's way of thinking. Communication is both cognitive (ideational) and social (relational), and learning how to argue in ways that build rather than destroy relationships is an important life skill (see section 1.2). The stronger the rapport between rhetor and audience, the greater the trust and the greater the likelihood of a win-win outcome. Wise rhetors pay close attention to cultural, ethical and interpersonal dynamics, as they practise active listening, knowing that *logos* needs to be catalysed by *pathos* and *ethos* to *win over* an audience.

5.3   Should I argue both sides?

In section 3.2, we considered **dyadic** and **triadic arguments**, based on whether arguers seek to persuade each other or a third-party audience. Aristotle's focus was on triadic argument, across all three genres of rhetoric that he discusses. In forensic, epideictic and deliberative rhetoric, arguments centre on questions of truth, value and policy, respectively. And, for Aristotle, the answer involved selecting one of two mutually exclusive positions (*A or not-A, but not both*).

Contemporary rhetors deciding whether or not to include opposing viewpoints in their texts typically consider their audience and the communication norms of their chosen genre. Some genres involve a division of labour, in which each party plays a pre-assigned role. For example, in a trial, the prosecutor's task is to prove guilt beyond reasonable doubt, while the defence attorney's task is to sow reasonable doubt in the minds of a third-party audience. Similarly, in debate competitions, each team argues just one side, arguing either for or against the motion, but not both.

If arguer's roles are not pre-assigned by generic convention, then rhetors need to consider their audience, when deciding whether or not to include opposing arguments. According to persuasion researcher Bert Bradley (1984, cited in Inch and Warnick, 2010, p.197), when audiences are favourably disposed to a message, a one-sided message is likely to be more effective. For, example if a speaker is proposing a new recycling initiative to an audience which supports recycling, it would only confuse the audience if the speaker began presenting arguments against recycling.

As persuasion consultant Harry Mills (2000) observes, if your audience is full of committed believers, they want you to rally them by reinforcing their beliefs and attitudes, not waste their time rehearsing dissenting views. In other words, with supportive audiences, rhetors are basically *preaching to the choir*, and the rhetor's task is to deliver an inspirational address that galvanises the audience into action, implementing the policy advocated by the rhetor. In short, what's needed in the acceptance knowing zone (see section 3.5) is a call-to-action, because audiences are not asking *WHY should I do what you're asking?* but *HOW can I do what you're asking*?

In contrast, a rhetor addressing either a neutral or a hostile audience cannot jump the gun but must first answer the audience's WHY question (*Why should I do what you're asking?*) before moving on to the HOW question (*How can I do what you're asking?*). With such audience, a **multi-sided argument** is more likely to work, for two reasons. First, acknowledging alternative viewpoints enhances the rhetor's *ethos* (trustworthiness) by projecting a well-informed and fair persona, reflecting expertise and integrity (see Figure 3.10).

Second, acknowledging alternative viewpoints produces an **inoculation effect**. When well-informed audiences encounter an argument, they will be thinking of objections to the rhetor's position. So, if rhetors anticipate and rebut these objections, they will, in effect, be inoculating the audience. Should the audience encounter the same objections in other contexts, they will find these less compelling, having already heard or read the rhetor's refutation of them. In short, just like people who've been vaccinated against a disease are less likely to fall prey to it, so also audiences who've had their objections answered are less likely to be swayed by these objections encountered elsewhere in the future.

5.4   Should I refute before or after the proof?

In classical oratory, the middle of a rhetor's speech (see Figure 5.1) comprised two parts: the **proof** (support for one's own stance) and the **refutation** (rebuttal of objections to one's stance). The Greek term for refutation *elenkhos* (questioning) can be understood as a process of rigorous testing of alternative views. In classical rhetoric, refutation followed proof, as speakers developed their own position, before addressing opposing views in order to demonstrate the strength of their own position. This pattern is still followed in **triadic arguments** (see section 3.2) such as the legal trial and academic debate.

When we engage in **dyadic argument**, however, it may be unwise to engage in refutation, particularly when addressing a hostile audience (see section 3.5), since rhetor and audience may have equally strong feelings about the issue being argued. Some hostile audiences may dislike the rhetor just because they don't share the same worldview, and may question the rhetor's open-mindedness. So, a direct attack on the audience's stance will not enhance rapport.

Mills (2000) advises rhetors facing hostile audiences to build rapport through humour and stories emphasising **common ground.** To enhance trustworthiness, he suggests using source material which the audience respects, and being scrupulously fair when citing facts and statistics. He recommends qualifying questionable claims using appropriate hedges (see section 3.9), and avoiding unsubstantiated claims altogether. Similarly, when using examples, Mills (2000) recommends using case studies and stories drawn from real life rather than hypothetical examples, since hostile audiences may perceive the latter as far-fetched and unrealistic.

Most importantly, Mills (2000) observes that it is far wiser to ask for a little and to get it than to ask for a lot and face rejection. To neutralise hostility, rhetors should emphasise a win-win outcome, the goal being to build bridges not walls. And, the measure of a rhetor's success is not full-scale conversion from active opposition to active support but reduced audience hostility so that they are not actively fighting (working against) the rhetor. As Mills (2000) put it, "they may not ever become a supporter, but the fact that they are no longer working against you must still be chalked up as a victory" (p.205).

5.5　Should I include all my arguments, even weak ones?

Including weak arguments when making a case just gives the audience rope to hang you with:

> Members of the audience who are predisposed to disagree with the arguer will be looking for reasons to discount the entire argument....If an argument seems invalid or insignificant, they will concentrate on it, frequently ignoring all other arguments. A week later, if someone asks them what the message was about, they may recall only the argument they found invalid.
> (Ruth Ann Clark, 1984, cited in Inch & Warnick 2010, p.198)

The second reason for not including weak arguments relates to Grice's Cooperative Principle. Philosopher of language H. Paul Grice (1972) envisaged conversation as a cooperative enterprise in which speakers follow unspoken rules or principles, which Grice dubbed **maxims** (see Figure 5.4).

Maxim	Defining Characteristic
Quality	*Be truthful* Don't lie or say that for which you have inadequate evidence
Quantity	*Be appropriately informative* Don't say more or less than is needed for the current purpose
Relation	*Be relevant to the current topic of conversation* Stay on topic
Manner	*Be brief and orderly* Avoid obscurity of expression and ambiguity

Figure 5.4　　Grice's maxims

The KISS acronym (*Keep It Short and Simple*) used by generations of writing teachers echoes Grice's Maxims. As Mills (2000) observes, "Most presenters overwhelm their audiences by drowning them in tidal waves of information" (p.133), despite the fact that most of us are incapable of absorbing, let alone remembering, the myriad messages we encounter daily.

Rhetors who are wise to the principle of selective attention recognise that people ignore most messages and focus on just a few key messages, usually one at a time. Accordingly, rhetors need to limit the number of points they make. As a general rule of thumb, Mills (2000) suggests that three to five points is plenty. The **rule of three** (see section 6.9) would suggest that three well-crafted points may be enough. The five-paragraph essay is in effect an embodiment of the rule of three, comprising three paragraphs each developing a key argument, book-ended by the opening and closing paragraphs of the essay.

5.6   Where should I place my strongest arguments?

Responsible rhetors brainstorm as many arguments as they can, then select only those arguments that their audience is likely to find most convincing. To do this, rhetors try to gauge the audience's level of knowledge, interest and support (see section 3.5 and Figure 5.5) as accurately as they can.

Audience	Persuasion Strategy
Neutral (neither supports nor opposes you, understands the issue but needs convincing)	• Draw heavily on concrete examples familiar to audience, and stories and analogies that appeal to their emotions. • Demonstrate your trustworthiness by acknowledging other points of view. • End by highlighting the downside of inaction or not accepting your proposal, and highlight benefits in terms of audience's priorities.
Uninterested (needs motivating and energizing)	• Grab their attention, using a story, headline or heart-stopping fact. • Show them how the topic affects or will affect them. • Support your case with 3-5 compelling facts supported by expert testimony or statistics.
Uninformed (doesn't have enough knowledge to be able to act, needs educating)	• Showcase your expertise (experience and qualifications). • Limit your message to three easy-to-follow logical points, supported by solid statistics and concrete examples. • Use anecdotes and an interactive style to create an emotional link to the issue.
Mixed (represents a spectrum of viewpoints)	• Identify who it is that you have to win over in terms of decision-makers and their advisers. • Don't promise everything to everyone because if there are groups with competing sub-agendas, you risk alienating everyone. • Where possible, appeal to the different groups in different parts of your message.

Figure 5.5   Customising your persuasion strategy (Mills, 2000, pp.202-4)

Having selected the best arguments for the audience and purpose at hand, the rhetor's next task is to decide how best to organise these. The **primacy-recency effect** (see section 3.6) suggests that rhetors should place their strongest argument at the beginning or the end of the message, not bury it in the middle. But, how does one decide whether to place the strongest argument first or last?

Mills (2000) suggests that when rhetors have to deliver a mixture of good news and bad news, they should put the **good news** first as it is likely to move the audience towards the rhetor, creating rapport that will make the audience more receptive to any bad news that follows. Mills (2000) also suggests that if the audience will make its decision immediately after hearing or viewing a persuasion message, then rhetors should position their strongest argument last because the recency-effect occurs immediately. In contrast, if an audience will make its decision only several days later, then rhetors are wiser to position their strongest argument first because the primacy-effect operates over longer stretches of time.

5.7   What shape should my argument take?

All *made* things are products of *tekhnê* (Greek for *art*) and have distinctive shapes. As with most things in life, there is no one 'correct' shape for a designed object. Instead, there is what Scott Crider (2005) labels **immanent design**, design features which emerge out of the purpose that the object will serve. To put it another way, form follows function. With discourse design, this means that communicative purpose influences the form of a message, at the level of rhetorical structure, coherence relations and lexico-grammar (see section 1.1).

Crider (2005, p.57) illustrates the idea of immanent design, using Andrew Marvel's (1621-1678) metaphysical poem "To His Coy Mistress". Marvel's text employs a form of argument that philosophers label a syllogism — an argument comprising two premises and a conclusion. So, it should perhaps come as no surprise that each element of the argument — major premise, minor premise and conclusion — occupies exactly one stanza each of Marvel's three-stanza poem, as outlined below:

Major Premise: *If we were immortal, then I would court you at leisure.*
Minor Premise: *We are not immortal.*
Conclusion: *Therefore, I cannot court you at leisure.*

In chapter 4, we considered an argument taxonomy based on the type of claim (truth, value or policy) being argued. Does each argument type display a particular design? To answer that question, we turn to the work of discourse analyst Michael Hoey (1983), who argues that human beings perceive coherence, or conceptual connections, in terms of matching and sequence clause relations. In other words, when we encounter two or more clauses (idea units), we look to see if they cohere by searching for matching relations of compatibility and contrast or (temporal and logical) sequence relations.

Matching clause relations are so-named because they entail pattern-matching, looking for constants (what stays the same) and variables (what changes). Do the clauses *My father loves bitter gourd. I hate it* cohere? Yes, they do, in a matching clause relation of contrast, signalled by the antonymous verbs *love* and *hate* expressing how my father and I feel about bitter gourd (see Figure 5.6).

	My father	*loves*	*bitter gourd.*
	I	*hate*	*it.*
Constant	family members	feeling about	bitter gourd
Variable	+father/-father	+love/-love	—

Figure 5.6   A 'contrast' matching relation

How about the clauses *My mother likes mangoes. I like them, too* — do they cohere? Yes, in a matching clause relation of compatibility (See Figure 5.7).

	My mother	*likes*	*mangoes.*
	I	*like*	*them, too.*
Constant	family members	like(s)	mangoes
Variable	+mother/-mother	—	—

Figure 5.7   A 'compatibility' matching relation

In short, when we say that a text is coherent, we're basically claiming that we can see the matching and/or sequence relations linking the clauses in that text. As Hoey (1983) emphasises, **coherence** (conceptual connectedness) resides not within a text but in the mind of the beholder, and depends on how information is organised in the perceiver's mind. This explains why a text may be coherent for one person but not another. Also, like most things in life, coherence is not an *all or nothing* phenomenon but a *more or less* experience.

Consider the clauses *John turned bright red. Peter was being a jerk.* Do they cohere? Most people see a causal relation between the two clauses, which can be unearthed through dialogue with the text (see Hoey, 1983), as illustrated below:

Text states: *John turned bright red.*

Reader asks: Why did John turn bright red?

Text answers: *Peter was being a jerk.*

To make explicit the coherence relations that they're seeing, language users employ **cohesive devices,** words and phrases which function as **discourse signals**, indicating matching and sequence clause relations in a text. For instance, we can signal the causal relation in the example above, using a subordinating conjunction: *John turned bright red* <u>*because*</u> *Peter was being a jerk.*

In their book-length study of cohesion in English, applied linguists Michael Halliday and Ruqaiya Hassan (1976) categorise cohesion in terms of the two broad word-classes (lexical and grammatical) found in English. **Lexical cohesion** results from the **repetition of lexical words** and **collocation**, analysed in terms of the semantic relations of:

❖ **Meronymy** (part-whole)   e.g. *leaf* is a meronym of the holonym *tree*

❖ **Hyponymy** (type-of)   e.g. *rose* is a hyponym of the superordinate *flower*

❖ **Synonymy** (similarity)   e.g. *begin* and *start*

❖ **Antonymy** (opposites)   e.g. *rich-poor, alive-dead, husband-wife*

Activity 5.2

Identify the lexical cohesion in the shampoo advertisement below.

[1] Timotei is mild to your hair and your scalp – so mild you can wash your hair as often as you like.
[2] Timotei cleans your hair gently, leaving it soft and shiny, with a fresh smell of summer meadows.

Comment on Activity 5.2

The ad uses both lexical repetition and collocation. The words *Timotei, hair,* and *mild* are repeated within and across sentences. The repetition of *Timotei* aids recall of the brand name; the repetition of *hair* is not surprising in the context of a shampoo ad; and, the repetition of *mild* emphasises a key feature of the shampoo. In terms of collocation, *hair* and *scalp* are co-meronyms of the holonym *head*, while *mild* and *gently* are synonymous, reinforcing the meaning 'not harsh'.

Grammatical cohesion in turn results from the use of grammatical words in four main devices, summarised in Figure 5.8, and exemplified in Figure 5.9.

Device	What it does	What to look for
Reference	refers anaphorically to a prior unit, or cataphorically to an upcoming unit	personal, possessive and demonstrative pronouns
Substitution	substitutes a longer unit with a shorter unit	words like *one, do, so, too,* and *the same,* replacing longer strings
Ellipsis	omits information recoverable from context	deleted prior information
Conjunction	signals matching or sequence relations	conjunctions (*e.g. and, or, but, so, thus, if, because, consequently*)

Figure 5.8   Grammatical cohesion

Device	Example
Reference	My nephew is a gifted musician. **He** plays the drums and guitar.
Substitution	I'd like an ice cream. Would you like **one, too**?
Ellipsis	Have you seen my glasses? No, I haven't. [… seen your glasses]
Conjunction	Sarah was tired. **So**, she went to bed.

Figure 5.9   Examples of grammatical cohesion

Activity 5.3

Do sentences (1) and (2) mean the same thing? How about sentences (3) and (4)? Paraphrase all four sentences so as to disambiguate them.

(1) *Jane got married and had a baby.*   (3) *John took a pill and felt unwell.*
(2) *Jane had a baby and got married.*   (4) *John felt unwell and took a pill.*

Comment on Activity 5.3

(1) *Jane got married before she had a baby.*
(2) *Jane got married after she had a baby.*
(3) *John felt unwell because he took a pill.*
(4) *John felt unwell. So, he took a pill.*

This activity highlights the ambiguity of the conjunction *and*, as reflected in the temporal (*before*, *after*) and causal (*because*, *so*) meanings implied in (1) to (4). The activity also points to the information value of sequential order. In (2), we infer that the baby was born out of wedlock, whereas in (1), we infer just the opposite because of the ordering of the two clauses. Similarly, in (3), we infer that the pill caused illness, whereas in (4), we see the pill as remedy because of the ordering of the clauses.

Matching clause relations and sequence clause relations form larger discourse patterns, such as the General-Particular and Problem-Solution text patterns, mentioned in chapter 4. **Policy arguments**, for instance, employ sequence clause relations within a larger Problem-Solution discourse pattern, given that Policy arguments must demonstrate the significant harm inherent to current policy (Problem) before introducing the remedy (Solution) (see section 4.7). **Definitional arguments**, meanwhile, employ matching (compatibility/contrast) clause relations within a larger General-Particular discourse pattern, in that definitions first identify the category of an entity, before detailing the traits distinguishing that entity from fellow members of the set (see section 4.5).

Activity 5.4

Hook's (1987) essay 'In Defence of Voluntary Euthanasia' is classically organised: Introduction (P1 to P2), Proof (P3-P5), Refutation (P6-P11) and Conclusion (P12-P13). Bearing in mind Hook's audience and rhetorical purpose, write a clear, concise and coherent 500-word analysis, justifying the changes you would make to Hook's organisation.

In Defense of Voluntary Euthanasia
Sidney Hook (*The New York Times*, March 1, 1987, p.49)

P1   A few short years ago, I lay at the point of death. A congestive heart failure was treated for diagnostic purposes by an angiogram that triggered a stroke. Violent and painful hiccups, uninterrupted for several days and nights, prevented the ingestion of food. My left side and one of my vocal cords became paralyzed. Some form of pleurisy set in, and I felt I was drowning in a sea of slime. At one point, my heart stopped beating; just as I lost consciousness, it was thumped back into action again. In one of my lucid intervals during those days of agony, I asked my physician to discontinue all life-supporting services or show me how to do it. He refused and predicted that someday I would appreciate the unwisdom of my request.

P2   A month later, I was discharged from the hospital. In six months, I regained the use of my limbs, and although my voice still lacks its old resonance and carrying power, I no longer croak like a frog. There remain some minor disabilities and I am restricted to a rigorous, low-sodium diet. I have resumed my writing and research.

P3   My experience can be and has been cited as an argument against honoring requests of stricken patients to be gently eased out of their pain and life. I cannot agree. There are two main reasons. As an octogenarian, there is a reasonable likelihood that I may suffer another "cardiovascular accident" or worse. I may not even be in a position to ask for the surcease of pain. It seems to me that I have already paid my dues to death — indeed, although time has softened my memories, they are vivid enough to justify my saying that I suffered enough to warrant dying several times over. Why run the risk of more?

P4   Secondly, I dread imposing on my family and friends another grim round of misery similar to the one my first attack occasioned.

P5   My wife and children endured enough for one lifetime. I know that for them the long days and nights of waiting, the disruption of their professional duties and their own familial responsibilities counted for nothing in their anxiety for me. In their joy at my recovery, they have been forgotten. Nonetheless, to visit another prolonged spell of helpless suffering on them as my life ebbs away, or even worse, if I linger into a comatose senility, seems altogether gratuitous.

P6   But what, it may be asked, of the joy and satisfaction of living, of basking in the sunshine, listening to music, watching one's grandchildren growing into adolescence, following the news about the fate of freedom in a troubled world, playing with ideas, writing one's testament of wisdom or folly for posterity? Is not all that one endured, together with the risk of recurrence, an acceptable price for the multiple satisfactions that are still open to a person of advanced years?

P7   Apparently those who cling to life no matter what, think so. I do not.

P8   The zest and intensity of these experiences are no longer what they used to be. I am not vain enough to delude myself that I can in the few remaining years make an important discovery useful for mankind or can lead to a social movement or do anything that will be historically eventful, no less event-making. My autobiography, which describes a record of intellectual and political experience of some historical value, already much too long, could be posthumously published. I have had my fill of joys and sorrows and am not greedy for more life. I have always thought that a test of whether one had found happiness in one's life is whether one would be willing to relive it—whether, if it were possible, one would accept the opportunity to be born again.

P9   Having lived a full and relatively happy life, I would cheerfully accept the chance to be reborn, but certainly not to be reborn again as an infirm octogenarian. To some extent, my views reflect what I have seen happen to the aged and stricken who have been so unfortunate as to survive crippling paralysis. They suffer, and impose suffering on others, unable even to make a request that their torment be ended.

P10   I am mindful, too, of the burdens placed upon the community, with its rapidly diminishing resources, to provide the adequate and costly services necessary to sustain the lives of those whose days and nights are spent on mattress graves of pain. A better use increases the opportunities and qualities of life for the young. I am not denying the moral obligation the community has to look after its disabled and aged. There are times, however, when an individual may find it pointless to insist on the fulfillment of a legal and moral right.

P11   What is required is no great revolution in morals but an enlargement of imagination and an intelligent evaluation of alternative uses of community resources.

P12   Long ago, Seneca observed that "the wise man will live as long as he ought, not as long as he can." One can envisage hypothetical circumstances in which one has a duty to prolong one's life despite its costs for the sake of others, but such circumstances are far removed from the ordinary prospects we are considering. If wisdom is rooted in knowledge of the alternatives of choice, it must be reliably informed of the state one is in and its likely outcome. Scientific medicine is not infallible, but it is the best we have. Should a rational person be willing to endure acute suffering merely on the chance that a miraculous cure might presently be at hand? Each one should be permitted to make his own choice—especially when no one else is harmed by it.

P13   The responsibility for the decision, whether deemed wise or foolish, must be with the chooser.

Activity 5.5

(1) Is White's essay an argument or a description? Justify your answer, clearly, concisely and coherently in 300 words or less.

(2) If White is making an argument, what is his main claim and where is it stated or implied? Answer clearly, concisely and coherently in 300 words or less.

Education
by E.B. White (March 1939, *Harper's* magazine)

P1   I have an increasing admiration for the teacher in the country school where we have a third-grade scholar in attendance. She not only undertakes her charges in all the subjects of the first three grades, but she manages to function quietly and effectively as a guardian of their health, their clothes, their habits, their mothers, and their snowball engagements. She has been doing this sort of Augean task for twenty years, and is both kind and wise. She cooks for the children on the stove that heats the room, and she can cool their passions or warm their soup with equal competence. She conceives their costumes, cleans up their messes, and shares their confidences. My boy already regards his teacher as his great friend, and I think tells her a great deal more than he tells us.

P2   The shift from city school to country school was something we worried about quietly all last summer. I have always rather favored public school over private school, if only because in public school you meet a greater variety of children. This bias of mine, I suspect, is partly an attempt to justify my own past (I never knew anything but public schools) and partly an involuntary defense against getting kicked in the shins by a young ceramist on his way to the kiln. My wife was unacquainted with public schools, having never been exposed (in her early life) to anything more public than the washroom of Miss Winsor's. Regardless of our backgrounds, we both knew that the change in schools was something that concerned not us but the scholar himself. We hoped it would work out all right. In New York our son went to a medium-priced private institution with semi-progressive ideas of education, and modern plumbing. He learned fast, kept well, and we were satisfied. It was an electric, colorful, regimented existence with moments of pleasurable pause and giddy incident. The day the Christmas angel fainted and had to be carried out by one of the Wise Men was educational in the highest sense of the term. Our scholar gave imitations of it around the house for weeks afterward, and I doubt if it ever goes completely out of his mind.

P3 His days were rich in formal experience. Wearing overalls and an old sweater (the accepted uniform of the private seminary), he sallied forth at morn accompanied by a nurse or a parent and walked (or was pulled) two blocks to a corner where the school bus made a flag stop. This flashy vehicle was as punctual as death: seeing us waiting at the cold curb, it would sweep to a halt, open its mouth, suck the boy in, and spring away with an angry growl. It was a good deal like a train picking up a bag of mail. At school the scholar was worked on for six or seven hours by half a dozen teachers and a nurse, and was revived on orange juice in mid-morning; In a cinder court he played games supervised by an athletic instructor, and in a cafeteria he ate lunch worked out by a dietitian. He soon learned to read with gratifying facility and discernment and to make Indian weapons of a semi-deadly nature. Whenever one of his classmates fell low of a fever the news was put on the wires and there were breathless phone calls to physicians, discussing periods of incubation and allied magic.

P4 In the country all one can say is that the situation is different, and somehow more casual. Dressed in corduroys, sweatshirt, and short rubber boots, and carrying a tin dinner-pail, our scholar departs at crack of dawn for the village school, two and a half miles down the road, next to the cemetery. When the road is open and the car will start, he makes the journey by motor, courtesy of his old man. When the snow is deep or the motor is dead or both, he makes it on the hoof. In the afternoons, he walks or hitches all or part of the way home in fair weather, gets transported in foul. The schoolhouse is a two-room frame building, bungalow type, shingles stained a burnt brown with weather-resistant stain. It has a chemical toilet in the basement and two teachers above stairs. One takes the first three grades, the other the fourth, fifth, and sixth. They have little or no time for individual instruction, and no time at all for the esoteric. They teach what they know themselves, just as fast and as hard as they can manage. The pupils sit still at their desks in class, and do their milling around outdoors during recess.

P5 There is no supervised play. They play cops and robbers (only they call it "Jail") and throw things at one another — snowballs in winter, rose hips in fall. It seems to satisfy them. They also construct darts, pinwheels, and "pick-up sticks" (jackstraws), and the school itself does a brisk trade in penny candy, which is for sale right in the classroom and which contains "surprises". The most highly prized surprise is a fake cigarette, made of cardboard, fiendishly lifelike.

P6 The memory of how apprehensive we were at the beginning is still strong. The boy was nervous about the change too. The tension, on that first morning in September when we drove him to school, almost blew the windows out of the sedan. And when later we picked him up on the road, wandering along with his little blue lunch-pail, and got his laconic report "All right" in answer to our inquiry about how the day had gone, our relief was vast. Now, after almost a year of it, the only difference we can discover in the two school experiences is that in the country he sleeps better at night — and *that* probably is more the air than the education. When grilled on the subject of school-in-country *vs.* school-in-city, he replied that the chief difference is that the day seems to go so much quicker in the country. "Just like lightning," he reported.

Comment on Activity 5.5

I would categorise White's essay as an explicit epideictic argument, celebrating the country school, and an implicit deliberative argument, supporting the ways of the country school, based on rhetorical analyst Jack Selzer's (2004) insightful discussion of the organisation of White's text. Drawing our attention to the opening and closing of the essay, Selzer notes how the essay begins and ends with favourable descriptions of the country school. As Selzer (2004) puts it, "the emphatic first and final positions of the essay are reserved for the virtues of the country school, while the account of the city school is buried in the unemphatic middle of the essay" (p.288). As Selzer astutely observes, the essay could have started with the second sentence of the second paragraph, promoting the city school, but doesn't.

Selzer also draws our attention to the body of White's essay, in which White moves from city to country, dealing with the city school all in one go before proceeding to the country school. As Selzer remarks, White could have used an "alternating" method of comparison, switching back and forth between the two schools. Or, he could have begun the body of this essay with the country school. Instead, White uses a comparative strategy of moving from inferior (*'this one is good'*) to superior (*but, this one is even better*)", allowing the organisation of his essay to subtly yet powerfully reinforce his epideictic purpose.

Having considered how arguers select their best arguments in chapter 4, in this chapter, we explored how rhetors organise the material they've selected, keeping in mind the three key factors of rhetorical purpose, audience and argument type. In chapter 6, we consider how rhetors style their arguments, selecting the best language (words and sentences) both to enact and amplify their arguments.

References

Connor, Ulla. (1996). *Contrastive rhetoric: Cross-cultural aspects of second-language writing.* Cambridge, UK: Cambridge University Press.

Creme, Phyllis and Lea, Mary R. (2008). *Writing at university: A guide for students* (3rd edition). Open University Press (McGraw Hill).

Crider, Scott F. (2005). *The Office of Assertion: An art of rhetoric for the academic essay.* Wilmington, Delaware: ISI Books.

Elbow, Peter. (2005). Bringing the rhetoric of assent and the believing game together—and into the classroom. *College English, 67*(4), 388–399.

Grice, H. Paul (1975). Logic and Conversation. In P. Cole and James L. Morgan (eds.) *Syntax and Semantics (vol.3) Speech Acts.* New York & London: Academic Press, pp.41-58.

Halliday, Michael and Hasan, Ruqaiya. (1976). *Cohesion in English*. London: Longman.

Hinds, John. (1983). Contrastive Rhetoric: Japanese and English. *Text 3*(2), pp. 183-195.

Hoey, Michael. (1983). *On the Surface of Discourse*. London: Allen & Unwin.

Inch, Edward S. and Warnick, Barbara. (2010). *Critical Thinking And Communication: The use of reason in argument* (6th edition). Boston: Allyn & Bacon.

Kaplan, Robert. (1966). Cultural Thought Patterns in Intercultural Education. *Language Learning 16*(1-2), 1-20.

Latour, Bruno and Woolgar, Steve. (1986). *Laboratory Life: The Social Construction of Scientific Facts.* Princeton University Press.

Mills, Harry. (2000). *Artful Persuasion: How to command attention, change minds, and influence people.* New York: AMACOM.

Ramage, John, Bean, John and Johnson, June. (2010). *Writing arguments: A rhetoric with readings* (8th ed.). New York: Longman.

Rogers, Carl. (1961). Communication: Its blocking and its facilitation. *On becoming a person* (pp.27–34). New York: Houghton.

Selzer, Jack. (2004). Rhetorical Analysis: Understanding how texts persuade readers. In Charles Bazerman & Paul Prior (eds.) *What writing does and how it does it: An introduction to analyzing texts and textual practices.* New Jersey: Lawrence Erlbaum, pp. 279-307.

Swales, John. (1990). *Genre analysis: English in academic and research settings.* Cambridge University Press.

Tubbs, Stewart L. (1968). Explicit versus implicit conclusions and audience commitment. *Speech Monographs 35* (1), pp. 14-19.

Chapter 6 Style

What do linguists and rhetoricians mean by style?

What parameters can we use to characterise style?

What's the difference between vernacular and technical styles?

What are some common tropes and schemes used by rhetors?

6.1   What do linguists mean by style?

We don't talk the same way to all people in all situations. Instead, we adopt different **personas** (see section 3.6) depending on WHOM we're speaking to, WHEN, WHERE, HOW and WHY (for what purpose). Just as we change our clothes depending on what we're doing and with whom (gardening with grandma or attending a friend's wedding), so also we adapt our language use to suit the context (see section 2.5).

So, when linguists use the term **style** (aka *register*), they mean a context-dependent variety of language emerging from the activity and people we're engaged with. Just as our dress style communicates something about who we are and how we wish to be perceived by others, so also linguistic or rhetorical style is a way of performing a textually-constructed social identity, or **persona** (see section 3.6). And, since identity is a relational construct, when rhetors perform a persona and style, they are in effect constructing a relationship with their audience, which can be analysed along the dimensions of **power differential** and **social distance** (see Figure 6.1).

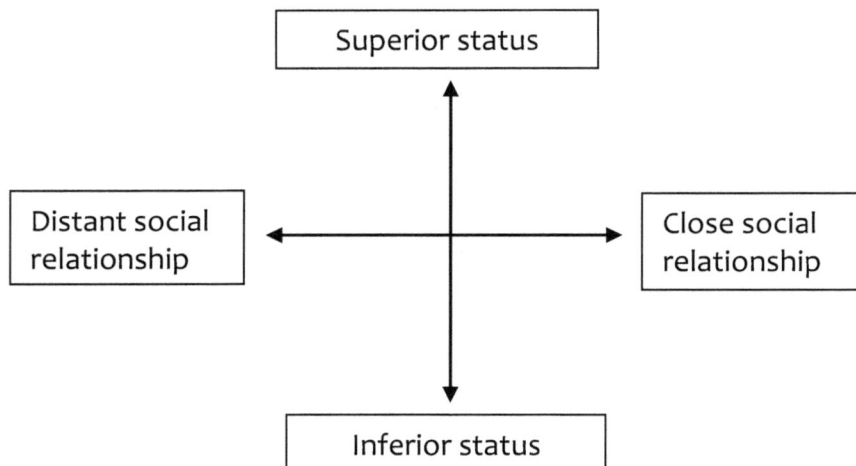

Figure 6.1   Power differential and social distance

Styles performed along the vertical **power differential** axis range from **formal** to **informal**, while styles performed along the horizontal **social distance** axis range from

impersonal to **personal**. Let's take a closer look at these style parameters, starting with the formal-informal continuum. Who would you be more informal with — (a) your best friend or (b) a visiting dignitary? Most people would choose (a) because close friendships tend to be more egalitarian than hierarchical, and we tend to be more informal with people we consider our peers, or equals. Conversely, we tend to be more formal with people we consider our social superiors.

Both formal and informal styles are recognisable in terms of lexico-grammatical features that we associate with each. **Informal style** (the linguistic counterpart of casual dress) is characterised by non-standard grammar, contractions, and solidarity markers like dialect, slang, and first-names and nick-names (see Figure 6.2).

Informal Style	Formal Style
Yo, dawg!	*Good Morning, Mrs Tan.*
Come with?	*Would you like to come with us?*
What ya doin'?	*What, may I ask, are you doing?*

Figure 6.2   Examples of formal and informal styles

Whereas the continuum of styles from formal to informal relates to power, the continuum of styles from personal to impersonal relates to social distance. One way to think about personal and impersonal styles is in terms of the distinction between talking TO and talking ABOUT. **Personal style** mirrors the social closeness we share with family and close friends, and tends to be *Me-You* or *We-You* oriented, employing ***address mode*** (first-person and second-person pronouns) to talk directly TO the audience. In contrast, **impersonal style** uses ***report mode*** to talk ABOUT people in the third-person (think of what a reporter does). Consider the two sentences below from an online faculty profile:

(1) *I received my PhD from the University of Birmingham.*

(2) *Professor Abraham received her PhD from the University of Birmingham.*

Which feels more personal? To me, (1) is more personal because it employs address mode to talk TO the audience in a *Me-You* dynamic characteristic of conversation. In contrast, sentence (2) talks ABOUT the faculty member in the third person (*her* rather than *my* PhD), distancing rather than drawing the audience into close association. Rhetors can obviously play with these stylistic parameters to achieve different rhetorical effects. **First-person narratives** typically draw an audience in, helping them identify with the narrator's viewpoint, in contrast to **third-person narratives** which create a sense of detached distance, or 'objectivity'. Personal and impersonal styles also help rhetors do face work: personal style creates or reinforces solidarity, while impersonal style mitigates imposition (see section 3.7), as illustrated by the directives below:

(a) *Patrons are reminded to switch of their mobile phones.*

(b) *You are reminded to switch off your mobile phones.*

Utterance (a) is less *in-your-face* than (b) because it strategically harnesses impersonal style, talking about patrons in third-person report mode (*their* rather than *your*) to minimise the imposition of the directive on addressees.

Activity 6.1

Rank the three sentences below from most to least impersonal, clearly identifying the lexico-grammatical features contributing to the stylistic effect perceived:

(a) *It was decided that the program should be terminated immediately.*

(b) *The committee decided to terminate the program immediately.*

(c) *We decided to terminate the program immediately.*

Commentary on Activity 6.1

For me, (a) is the most impersonal, and (c), the least impersonal. Two features —pronoun choice and passivisation — seem to contribute to this effect. Utterance (c) uses first-person active voice, mirroring the *We-You* dynamic of conversation. In contrast, (b) uses active voice, but in third-person report mode, replacing the human and personal *We* with an impersonal institutional agent, *the committee.* Sentence (a) not only passivises utterance (c) but uses an **agentless passive** (deleting the agent of the verb *terminate*), thereby removing human agency from the picture altogether.

Activity 6.2

Texts 1 and 2 represent the opening words of Aldous Huxley's and Joshua Fishman's books on language. Rhetoricians Wayne Booth and Gregory Marshall (1991, p.285) ask readers to consider three questions about these openings:

1. Which author makes you more inclined to continue travelling in his company?

2. Which writer projects a more appealing character?

3. Quite apart from whether you're much interested in reading about language, which author seems the more interesting person?

Text 1
Words and their meanings — this is the subject that I have chosen. Some of you, no doubt, will wonder at my choice; for the subject will strike you as odd and unimportant, even rather silly. This is quite understandable. For a long time past, thinking men have tended to adopt a somewhat patronizing attitude towards the words they use in communicating with

their fellows and formulating their own ideas. "What do you read, my lord?" Polonius asked. And with all the method that was in his madness Hamlet scornfully replied, "Words, words, words." That was at the beginning of the seventeenth century; and from that day to this the people who think themselves realists have gone on talking about words in the same contemptuous strain.

There was a reason for this behaviour — at least an excuse. Before the development of experimental science, words were too often regarded as having magical significance and power. With the rise of science a reaction set in, and for the last three centuries words have been unduly neglected as things having only the slightest importance.... We talk about "mere matters of words" in a tone which implies that we regard words as things beneath the notice of a serious-minded person.

This is a most unfortunate attitude. For the fact is that words play an enormous part in our lives and are therefore deserving of the closes study....

(Aldous Huxley, 1940, *Words and their meaning*)

Text 2

Professional linguists have long been aware that languages differ from each other in many patterned respects. Similarly, professional sociologists have long been aware that societies differ from each other in many patterned respects. However, for several reasons, there has thus far been too little realization in either camp that language and society reveal various kinds and degrees of patterned co-variation. The sociology of language represents one of several recent approaches to the study of patterned co-variation of language and society. Under "language" one may be concerned with different codes..., and social class varieties of a particular regional variant..., stylistic varieties related to levels of formality, etc. Each of these varieties may be studied....

(Joshua A. Fishman, 1977, *Readings in the sociology of language*)

Booth and Marshall's (1991, p. 286) comment

While both of these beginnings tell us about the authors' topics, each one simultaneously portrays a radically different picture of the author who is speaking. The first brings himself on in the very first sentence with an "I", and with a direct engagement of the reader's imagined resistance to his topic. He keeps himself on stage throughout, speaking directly and openly, as one person to another. He sounds not like a distanced scholar but like a teacher who conveys a sense of urgency about his interest in words....he portrays himself as a person who can describe complicated issues concretely and clearly. The reader can tell that the writer is thinking hard as a writer about how to make himself clear to his reader ,not just how to remain accurate about his subject.

Reading the second author, in contrast, we can't be sure that he is picturing his reader at all. He seems to have no sense of responsibility for making himself engaging, or for caring whether his reader will have trouble following what he says. Perhaps quite unconsciously, he adopts what he would no doubt describe as a standard "scholarly voice". He tries to keep himself offstage, writing sentences that seem to be uttered by sociological truth itself, with no human intervention. He steadily and self-consciously repeats his matter-of-fact descriptive terms, and he seems comfortable being a "one", rather than an "I" or a "we".

Pronoun choices affect *ethos* in terms of projecting a consistent *persona*, or *voice*, without fakery or hypocrisy in a way that inspires trust. Psychotherapist Carl Rogers (1961) labels this quality **congruence**, being comfortable with oneself in the role one has assumed. When analysing style, rhetorical analysts typically discuss two key terms: voice and tone. **Voice** refers to the persona or identity adopted over the entire length of the persuasion message, whereas **tone** refers to the rhetor's attitude towards the audience and issue being discussed.

Rhetoricians Wayne Booth and Gregory Marshall explain the relationship between voice and tone in terms of the human face and the expressions it wears:

> voice is to one's writing as face is to one's identity, while tone is the expression on the face, a transitory kind of presence that changes to suit different occasions.... As your face goes from expressions of anger to peacefulness to amusement to contempt to quizzical to animated to sleepy to bored to shifty to frightened to sad to determined and to a score of others that you may assume in the course of any given day, it still remains recognizably your face and recognizably distinct.... Your voice in writing...announces a kind of identity that you create as you write. Your writing voice *is* your writing identity, just as your face *is* your physical identity...and both can go through an enormous range of expressions without losing their distinctiveness.
>
> (Booth & Marshall, 1991, p. 287)

To project the appropriate voice and tone, rhetors make strategic choices in terms of both WHAT they say and HOW they say it by drawing on the lexico-grammatical resources afforded by language. For example, rhetors can employ the first-person pronoun throughout an argument or shift into first-person mode only at those points where they wish to create a heightened sense of intimacy or candour.

The plural first-person pronoun *we* is particularly tricky, given that English *we* is ambiguous. It can include the audience (*we = you and me*) or exclude it (*we = me and someone else*). Used ethically, **audience-inclusive *we*** can unite rhetor and audience in a community of shared belief. Used manipulatively, it could result in a hostile audience responding *Please don't presume to speak for me!* The pronoun *we* can also cause confusion if its referent cannot be recovered from the linguistic or situational context, causing the audience to wonder *Who is this 'we' you keep referring to?*

To recap, personal style reduces social distance, drawing the audience into the unfolding action and engaging interest, interactively. Compare (1) to (3):

(1)   *If one were to be abroad for years, one would spot the changes in Singapore more easily.*

(2)   *If readers were to be abroad for years, they would spot the changes in Singapore more easily.*

(3)   *If you were to be abroad for years, you would spot the changes in Singapore more easily.*

Did sentence (3) draw you in more than (1) and (2)? We can use politeness norms to explain this rhetorical effect. When someone addresses us, positive politeness demands that we show our respect by giving the addresser our full attention. Ignoring people when they're talking to us would threaten the speaker's positive face needs.

In contrast, if our purpose is to deliver bad news, e.g. complaints and negative judgements, impersonal style is less face-threatening.

  (a) I was troubled by your paper's assertion that….

  (b) I was troubled by *The Straits Times'* assertion that….

The second-person pronoun in sentence (a) above creates a *Me vs. You* dynamic, which could be interpreted as the rhetorical equivalent of wagging an accusatory finger in someone's face — not something people enjoy being on the receiving end of!

Activity 6.3

The examples below are from John Mauk's (2006, p.54) book *Inventing Arguments*. Using what you've learnt about personal-impersonal and formal-informal styles, analyse the writer's *ethos* coherently in 500 words or less.

Text 1
The university should shovel and salt the sidewalks in the early morning before classes begin, not later that afternoon. You just about kill yourself, slipping and sliding to class through the snow. You're bound to be late for biology, which you're already failing.

Text 2
The university should shovel and salt the sidewalks in the early morning before classes begin, not later that afternoon. I just about kill myself, slipping and sliding to class through the snow. I'm bound to be late for biology, which I'm already failing.

Text 3
The university should shovel and salt the sidewalks in the early morning before classes begin, not later that afternoon. Students and faculty could be seriously injured, scurrying to class in such hazardous conditions.

6.2   Instrumentalities: medium, mode and channel

In Hymes's (1972) SPEAKING mnemonic (see Figure 2.4), the letter *I* represents instrumentalities, by which Hymes meant the linguistic code (the particular language variety) and the channel (speech or writing) used to communicate. I prefer broadening the term to encompass how messages are produced (**mode**), disseminated (**medium**) and received (**channel**) — See Figure 6.3.

INSTRUMENTALITIES	CHOICES AVAILABLE
Mode of production *How is the text produced?*	Spoken Written
Medium of dissemination *How is the text disseminated?*	Print Broadcast (radio, television, film) Online
Channel of reception *How is the text received?*	Auditory (ears) Visual (eyes) Audiovisual (eyes and ears)

Figure 6.3   Instrumentalities – medium, mode and channel

The main reason for considering medium, mode and channel when analysing style is that communication today tends to be highly mediated. Unlike classical rhetors who relied primarily on face-to-face communication, contemporary rhetors can disseminate their persuasion messages through a wide array of communication platforms, including print, broadcast (radio, television, film) and online **media** received through the ears, eyes or both. Radio, for instance employs only the auditory channel, unlike television which employs both auditory and visual channels.

Of the two modes of communication, speech and writing, speech is the older. But, it is also ephemeral. So, oral communities (communities without writing systems) tend to rely on repetition (telling the old stories over and over again) as a means of storing and transferring knowledge from one generation to the next. Today, of course, we use video recorders and digital software packages of various kinds to archive speech. In that sense, writing represents the oldest technology invented to record and retrieve speech. And, once writing appeared on the scene, communicators had to decide whether or not to *script* speech.

Unscripted speech is unplanned and spontaneous, characterised by hesitations, false starts and other processing errors which are typically removed during transcription and editing, prior to written publication. The prototypical example of spontaneous speech is face-to-face conversation, which differs from writing in two main ways. First, face-to-face conversation tends to be highly contextualised and synchronous, in that both conversational partners are co-present in time and space, sharing the same context (sights, sounds and surroundings).

In contrast, writers and readers tend usually to be separated by time and space. Think about letters received from different parts of the world or books written hundreds of years ago that we still read today. Because reading and writing tend to be **asynchronous** activities, writers have to be far more explicit than speakers, when referring to persons, places and events. Unlike conversational partners who can point at things in their shared context, writers have to state the referents of **deictic words** (words like *his, hers, here, there, these, those* marking personal, spatial and temporal orientation, whose referents are context-bound). Think of a lady buying cold meats at the delicatessen saying, *Could I have a hundred grams of that* [pointing to the shaved ham], *please?* If the same transaction had to be carried out via a written note, the referent of the demonstrative pronoun *that* would have to be stated (explicitly identified).

Secondly, speech and writing differ in terms of processing speeds and constraints. When we speak extemporaneously, we're basically thinking on our feet. There isn't much time to plan or rehearse complicated lexico-grammatical patterns. Listeners in turn typically get just one chance to catch an utterance, unless speakers repeat what they say. As a result of the processing constraints faced by speakers and listeners, spoken sentences tend to be linked together like a string of pearls, in a ***paratactic*** syntactic pattern (two or more independent clauses linked by **coordinating conjunctions** to form a **compound sentence**).

Writing, in contrast, generally allows writers more time to draft and revise messages, the exception being instant chat or hastily written notes, which may contain slips of the fingers, akin to slips of the tongue in speech. Readers, conversely, can re-read what they don't understand, as long as they have continued access to the written text. Consequently, written sentences tend to nest clauses, like Russian dolls or Chinese boxes, in a ***hypotactic*** syntactic pattern (one or more dependent clauses embedded within a main clause by **subordinating conjunctions** to form a **complex sentence**).

If you revisit Activity 5.5, you'll notice that the sentences of E. B. White's essay reflect the canonical **Subject Verb Object** order of spoken English, with Subject and Verb positioned closely together. There are only seven instances of ***hypotaxis*** in the entire essay — two instances in the first and third paragraphs, and five in the second paragraph. If you think that is not a low ratio of hypotaxis:parataxis, compare it with a 1000-word essay of your own.

> When White does add length to a sentence, he does it not by adding complex clauses that modify other clauses, but by adding independent clauses (ones that begin with "and" or "but" — what classical rhetoricians calls ***parataxis***) and by adding modifiers and phrases in parallel series. Some examples? The teacher is a guardian "of their health, their clothes, their habits, their mothers, and their snowball engagements"; the boy "learned fast, kept well, and we were satisfied"; the bus "would sweep to a halt, open its mouth, suck the boy in, and spring away."

And so forth. The "ands" make White's essay informal and conversational, never remote or scholarly.

(Selzer, 2004, p.290, italics and bold in original)

As we analyse the influence of instrumentalities on style, it's important to remember that messages can **cross over** from one medium, mode or channel to another. The adage *Not words on a page, but people on a stage* underscores the fact that play scripts although written, are not usually meant to be read silently but to be heard, and therefore display the characteristics of the spoken rather than written mode. Campaign speeches and conference presentations, similarly, are written to be heard. To make the listener's task easier, these texts typically favour parataxis over hypotaxis, unlike their *written-to-be-read* counterparts (policy documents and research articles).

6.3   Vernacular, public and technical styles

In section 2.8, we considered Thomas Goodnight's (1982) categorisation of **argument spheres** into personal, public and technical. We can in fact broaden this concept to encompass **activity spheres**, distinguishing between private, public and technical spheres (see Figure 6.4).

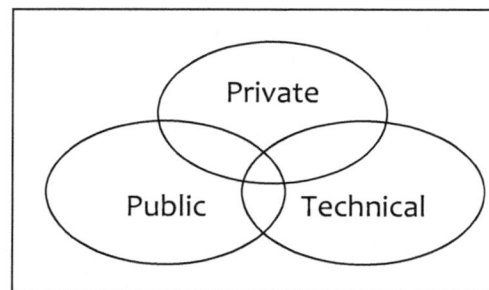

Figure 6.4   Private, public and technical activity spheres

The **private activity sphere** encompasses private communication between family and close friends. In contrast, the **public activity sphere** encompasses all communicative activity occurring under the public gaze. The **technical activity sphere** in turn involves communication between fellow specialists about their shared area of expertise. Not surprisingly, each sphere has a preferred style (private, public or technical), based on the audiences and activities engaged with, as summarised in Figure 6.5.

Preferred Style	Activity Sphere	Audience
Vernacular	Private	family and close friends
Public	Public	members of the public
Technical	Technical	fellow specialists

Figure 6.5   Vernacular, public and technical styles

Activity 6.4

Which sounds more vernacular to you — (a) or (b), and why?

(a) *Plants vary lots in how they grow.* (b) *Plant growth exhibits significant variation.*

Comment on Activity 6.4

To me, (a) sounds more vernacular than (b). Vernacular style describes people doing things, using everyday words. Sentence (a) follows this pattern, talking about what plants do, using words familiar to most English speakers. In contrast, sentence (b) talks about an abstraction (*plant growth*), using Latinate lexis (*significant* instead of *lots*, *exhibits*), and nominalising actions (*vary* becomes *variation*).

According to rhetorician Richard Lanham (2003) **vernacular style** tends to be a **verb style** that conveys a sense of action by adopting the canonical Subject Verb Object order of active English sentences. In contrast, **technical style** favours a **noun style**, characterised by **nominalisation** (the process of turning verbs into nouns, thereby conveying stasis rather than action) and **passivisation** (using passive voice, particularly agentless passives to delete human agency).

To illustrate the difference between the two styles, Lanham (2003) offers two versions of the famous quote attributed to Caesar (p.11).

> **Verb style**   *I came. I saw. I conquered*
>
> **Noun style**   *Arrival. Reconnaissance. Victory.*

According to Lanham, Britain's World War II Prime Minister Winston Churchill underscored the difference between verb style and noun style when he allegedly censured a visiting general's nominalised style: "What if I had said — instead of — "We shall fight on the beaches" — "Hostilities will be engaged with our adversary on the coastal perimeter"?' (p.11). As Lanham explains, "Churchill wanted to depict a Britain *acting*, on the attack, not stymied in bureaucratic defensiveness" (*ibid.*).

Technical style welcomes a noun style because technical communication tends to be concept-driven, seeking to give us the 'facts' in a detached manner implying ineluctable truth. This is a style in which things happen without human agency. And, nominalisation and passivisation are the syntactic resources which technical writers employ to create this rhetorical effect of a rule-governed world in which phenomena occur without the intervention of human agents).

STYLE	EXAMPLE	OBSERVATION
Vernacular	*I found him incompetent.* *So, I fired him.*	uses dynamic verbs (*found, fired*) and active voice
Technical	*Appropriate action was initiated on the basis of systematic discussion indicating that the termination process would be appropriate.*	uses agentless passive (*was initiated*) and nominalises verbs (*action, discussion, termination*)

Figure 6.6   **Examples of vernacular and technical styles**

As Lanham (2003) observes, noun-style syntax tends to follow the syntactic pattern **Noun Phrase (NP) + link verb + Prepositional Phrase (PP)**, as illustrated in Figure 6.7.

Noun Style syntax NP + link verb + PP	Verb Style syntax NP + transitive verb + NP
*This sentence **is** in need of an active verb.* (9 words)	*This sentence needs an active verb.* (6 words)

Figure 6.7   **Noun style and verb style syntax**

Notice how the [link verb + PP] construction lengthens sentences unnecessarily, violating Grice's Maxim of Manner, bidding us to be brief (see section 5.5), increasing what Lanham calls the **lard factor** (empty padding). In the example above, the [link verb + PP] construction increases the lard factor by 33%, using nine rather than six words.

Thus far, we've considered how vernacular and technical styles differ syntactically. But, the two styles also differ lexically because of the evolution of the English language (to view 1600 years of linguistic history condensed into ten minutes, look for The Open University video *The History of English in Ten Minutes* on YouTube). English began life as a Germanic language, then added a large Latinate lexicon to its word stock because of two historical events:

❖ England's conversion to Roman Christianity in 957 AD (Latin was the language of the Roman Church); and,

❖ the Norman Invasion of 1066 AD (the Normans spoke an early version of French, a daughter language of Latin).

As a result, the everyday words we use tend to draw from the Germanic word stock, whereas the vocabulary we use in the more specialised spheres of education, law, church and state comes from the Latinate lexicon, as illustrated below.

GERMANIC WORDS	LATINATE EQUIVALENTS
think, see	*conceive, perceive*
alive	*animate*
freedom	*liberty*

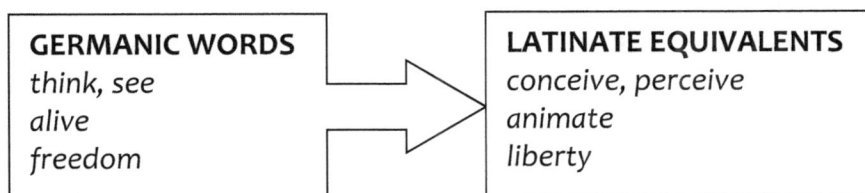

To recap, technical and vernacular styles can be distinguished in terms of both lexis and syntax, as summarised in Figure 6.8.

STYLE	LEXICO-GRAMMATICAL FEATURES
Technical	❖ Arcane words with Latin or Greek roots ❖ Noun style featuring nominalisation and passivisation
Vernacular	❖ Familiar everyday words with Germanic roots ❖ Verb style featuring dynamic verbs and active voice

Figure 6.8   Lexico-grammatical features of vernacular and technical styles

Activity 6.5

Consider these two utterances:
(1) *She has bruises and several cuts.*
(2) *She suffered a hematoma and several lacerations.*
Who might utter these words, to whom, when, where and for what purpose?

Activity 6.6

Compare the two texts below. The first is an excerpt from a research article; the second is a rewrite of the first by an animal rights activist. How would you characterise the communicative purpose, audience and style of each?

Original text
Following these injections, shivering began within a minute or two and quickly became vigorous and widespread. The next effect was vocalisation. It began with periods of meowing which became more frequent and of longer duration and gradually the meowing changed to growling and yelping. Later tachypnoea (rapid breathing), panting, salivation, piloerection (hair standing on end) and ear twitching were observed; later again, periods of intense excitation alternated with periods of a more restful condition.
(Source: a paper by Wilhelm Feldberg on an experiment on the effects of injecting a mustard drug into the brains of cats. *British Journal of Pharmacology*, 1978)

Rewrite by animal rights activist

The scientist plunges the syringe full of mustard gas into the cat's brain. In minutes, the tiny cat is shivering and mewing pitifully. As the pain intensifies, she whimpers and yelps then screams. Calmly, the scientist watches as his defenceless victim gasps, drools and twitches, her hair on end as she thrashes wildly about. Eventually, she subsides, exhausted, only to resume her agonised thrashing, as the cruel experiment goes on and on and on.

6.4   What do rhetoricians mean by style?

In the previous section we saw how linguists view style as a means of doing *ethos*, by performing a **persona** adapted to the audience and rhetorical purpose at hand. By adaptively employing the lexico-grammatical features associated with formal-informal, personal-impersonal and public-vernacular-technical styles, rhetors can create a hierarchical or egalitarian relationship with their audience, increase intimacy or social distance, and address the audience as fellow specialists or not.

How do rhetoricians view style? If you look back at the five canons of rhetoric (see section 4.1), you'll notice that Aristotle, Cicero and Quintilian explored the canons of style and invention separately, which has led some people to mistakenly view style as an ornamental extra, a decorative detail added after invention.

But, as we know, style and substance (WHAT we say and HOW we say it) are inextricably linked (see section 2.6). Rhetoricians view style as a means of underscoring and amplifying one's message, of making key points salient through marked lexical and syntactic choices, known as ***tropes*** and ***schemes***, respectively. (To view some of the hundreds of tropes and schemes categorised by classical and renaissance rhetoricians, visit the online rhetoric *Silva Rhetoricae* by Professor Gideon Burton of Brigham Young University).

Fundamentally, tropes and schemes project significance by producing **framing effects** that **skew perception** in predictable ways. Have a look at the two *central* circles below. Does one seem larger than the other?

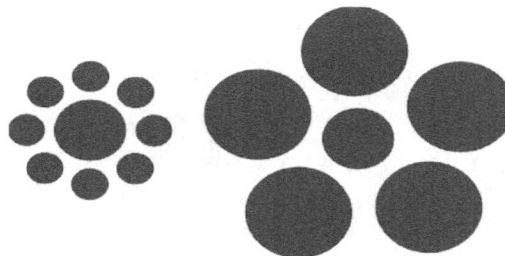

If you answered *Yes*, you've just demonstrated that significance is relative — that things seem big, small or medium, i.e. important, trivial or something in between, based on how they're framed. Here's how the optical illusion works: The central circle on the left is surrounded by circles smaller than itself, making the central circle seem larger by contrast. The central circle on the right, meanwhile, is surrounded by larger circles than itself, making it seem smaller by comparison. The net result is that the central circle on the left seems larger than that on the right, even though they're both identical in size.

A similar framing effect can be achieved linguistically via marked lexical and syntactic choices — tropes and schemes. Words are the short-hand labels that we use to name concepts. Rhetors employ tropes (marked lexical choices) to foreground the concepts they wish to emphasise, harnessing denotation and connotation, euphemism and dysphemism, and literal and figurative meaning, respectively. For maximum rhetorical impact, these tropes are organised into schemes, comprising two-part and three-part patterns of repetition and contrast (see sections 6.8 and 6.9).

6.5 Tropes: denotation and connotation

As we discuss tropes, keep asking yourself, *What's in a label?* As Shakespeare put it, *Would a rose by any other name smell as sweet?* The words we use to describe things (people, places, experiences, events, etc.) can skew our perception of those things because words don't just convey concepts (denote meaning), they also evoke emotional associations (carry positive and negative connotations). Dictionaries tend to list the denotative meanings of words, noting connotation mainly for **taboo words** likely to give offense (see section 6.6).

Both denotation and connotation, like language use in general, are context-dependent. For example, the words *vision* and *sight* can be used interchangeably to complete the sentence *I have good _____.* They're **synonymous**, having the same denotation and a fairly neutral connotation. Now consider the utterance *What a _____ she looked!* While it's still possible to fill the slot with either *vision* or *sight*, the two words are no longer synonymous because they have completely antithetical connotations, *vision* being positively-laden and *sight* being negatively-laden, in this context.
In the late 1940s, the British philosopher Bertrand Russell playfully conjugated the verb *be* on a BBC radio program as follows: *I am firm; you are obstinate; he is a pig-headed fool*, concisely illustrating the power of words to convey both ideas (denotation) and attitudes (connotation). Effective communicators clearly harness the synergy between denotation and connotation to achieve specific rhetorical goals.

Activity 6.7

Do Extracts 1 and 2 mean the same — why (not)?

Extract 1

O, for a draught of vintage! that hath been
Cooled for a long age in the deep-delvèd earth!"

Extract 2

O, for a drink of wine that has been reduced in temperature over a long period in ground with deep furrows in it!

> **Comment on Activity 6.7**
>
> Extract 1 is from John Keats' poem "Ode to Autumn", while Extract 2 is William Alston's (1964) paraphrase of Keats. As Monroe Beardsley (1970, p.54) observes, by selecting the word "vintage", Keats is in effect both describing and praising the wine, given that "vintage" connotes both old wine and good wine.

Connotations range from the fairly neutral (slightly coloured with feeling) to extremely positive or negative. Semanticist Richard Weaver (1990) refers to words with positive connotations as *purr words* (aka *god words*) and those with negative connotations as *snarl words* (aka *devil words*).

Activity 6.8

Here are some examples of purr words and snarl words — which is which? Justify your answer, clearly concisely, and coherently!

> *truth, patriot, family, choice, traitor, coerce, flag, love, hate, friendship*

What other examples of purr words and snarl words can you think of?

6.6 Tropes: euphemisms and dysphemisms

Most cultures have norms governing social behaviour which include **linguistic taboos** (from Polynesian *tapu*) prohibiting the mention of entities and experiences that the community considers either sacred or profane. To get round this ban, speakers use **euphemisms** (from Greek *euphanai* 'to speak fair or well') to replace taboo words. For example, a speaker might say *went to the bathroom* instead of *defecated* and *passed away* instead of *died*.

Used appropriately, euphemisms form part of a community's social contract concerning polite behaviour (see section 3.7), and stem from a desire to spare others' feelings, in contrast to **dysphemisms** which spring from the opposite motivation. Rhetors employ euphemisms and dysphemisms to frame things positively or negatively, to show respect or disrespect. The abortion debate, for instance, has produced euphemisms labelling support for abortion as *pro-choice* as well as dysphemisms labelling abortionists as *baby killers* to skew audience attitudes towards praise and blame, respectively.

As with most things in life, euphemistic language has its dark side in that it can degenerate into doublespeak and politically correct speech. **Doublespeak** refers to the use of euphemistic language not to spare people's finer feelings but to whitewash reality by hiding the human and moral costs of the actions described. *The Quarterly Journal of Doublespeak* (cited in Lutz 1996, pp. 118-119) offers the following examples: *downsizing* and *employee repositioning* for firing people at will; *strategic misrepresentation, reality augmentation* and *terminological inexactitudes* for lies told by politicians.

Politically correct speech in turn typically begins life as a well-meaning attempt to avoid giving offence (see politeness norms in section 3.7), by replacing demeaning or negative labels with more positive ones. But, the term itself has taken on negative connotations, and is seen in some quarters as an attempt to sugarcoat reality. Obviously, what counts as *politically correct* will vary from one socio-historical context to the next, since words undergo changes to denotation and connotation.

In terms of denotation, the scope of a word can broaden or narrow, undergoing **semantic broadening** or **narrowing**. The word *virgin*, for example, used to mean unmarried maiden, but has undergone semantic broadening to include both men and women in contemporary usage. In contrast, the word *meat* has undergone semantic narrowing in that it used to mean food generally (as in *meat and drink*) but now refers to a specific kind of food (the flesh of animals).

In terms of connotation, words can become more positive or negative over time, undergoing **amelioration** or **pejoration**. For example, *knights* and *villains* were medieval servants, but whereas *knight* has undergone amelioration, *villain* has undergone pejoration. When words undergo pejoration to the point that they become so offensive as to be considered **taboo**, they get replaced by new words, which similarly undergo a process of amelioration or pejoration. The table below shows the clinical terms used to describe people with low IQ scores in the first half of the twentieth century. Over time, these words acquired such strongly pejorative meanings that they are no longer used in clinical psychology today.

IQ Score	Mental deficiency	Mental retardation
50-69	*moron*	mild
35-49	*imbecile*	moderate
20-34		severe
below 20	*idiot*	profound

source: http://www.iqcomparisonsite.com/IQBasics.aspx

6.7   Tropes: figures of speech

Most of the time, we communicate literally about concrete entities doing concrete things, e.g. *Sarah hugged Joel.* At other times, we choose to speak figuratively, using tropes known as **figures of speech** (see Figure 6.9).

Figure of speech	What it does
Simile	compares two essentially unlike things in a phrase introduced by *as* or *like* (e.g. *My love is like a river.*)

Metaphor	implicitly compares two essentially unlike things (e.g. *The fog comes on little cat feet.*)
Metonymy	uses a closely-associated concept to name something (e.g. referring to a rich man as *money bags*)
Synecdoche	uses a part to name the whole (e.g. referring to a car as *wheels*)
Personification	endows non-humans with human qualities (e.g. *I can hear freedom whispering*)
Pun	plays on word meanings (e.g. *an ambassador is someone who lies abroad for his country*)
Irony	saying one thing and meaning just the opposite
Understatement	underplays an idea (e.g. describing a deep gash as *just a scratch*)
Hyperbole	exaggerates an idea (e.g. *I'm so hungry I could eat a horse!*)

Figure 6.9   Nine common figures of speech

Of the two figures of speech, *simile* and *metaphor,* **metaphors** carry a higher cognitive load because unlike similes, metaphors leave it to the audience to infer the basis as well as the purpose of the comparison. To understand the difference, compare utterances (a) and (b) below:

Simile	Metaphor
(a) *Sarah sailed down the corridor like a stately galleon.*	(b) *Sarah sailed down the corridor.*

Sentence (a) makes explicit the comparison between Sarah's movement and that of a stately galleon in a simile introduced by the word *like*. In contrast, (b) requires us to decide whether or not to interpret the verb *sailed* literally. If we discover that Sarah didn't literally sail down the corridor, we move on to a figurative interpretation which invites us to envisage Sarah as a sailing vessel of some sort.

Why do rhetors use figures of speech? Here's how Max Atkinson explains it:

> A picture may sometimes tell a thousand words, but words can just as easily be used to create a thousand images. Whether it's '*an iron curtain descending*' across Europe (Winston Churchill), '*a wind of change blowing* across Africa' (Harold Macmillan) or '*a great beacon light of hope shining* across America' (Martin Luther

King) we know instantly that the speaker is not speaking literally, and have no trouble in seeing exactly what is meant. And, *'seeing'* the point is a crucial part of the process because the use of imagery requires listeners to make the connection between the visual image and he reality to which it refers, and then to draw their own conclusion. The mental effort involved in doing this coupled with the satisfaction that can come from seeing the point, may well be at the heart of why the use of imagery is such an effective way to strike chords with an audience.

(Atkinson, 2004, p.215, italics in original)

In short, imagery enables rhetors to paint with words, encapsulating complex ideas concisely and vividly. But, language today also contains lots of dead metaphors, stock phrases and clichés that have lost their novelty. Rhetors who employ these timeworn slogans unthinkingly may be perceived as lazy and manipulative, especially by hostile audiences (see section 3.5) because buzzwords can and often do short-circuit creative and critical thinking by triggering knee-jerk responses. For example, it's fairly common in the abortion debate to hear abortionists being described as baby killers, but is the comparison warranted? For that, we would need to consider how exactly abortion is similar to/different from infanticide.

Activity 6.9

The excerpt below is from US President George H. Bush's (1989) inaugural address. What tropes do you see, and how do they affect our perception of Bush's *ethos*? Answer clearly, concisely and coherently in 300 words or less.

I come before you and assume the Presidency at a moment rich with promise. We live in a peaceful, prosperous time, but we can make it better. For a new breeze is blowing, and a world refreshed by freedom seems reborn; for in man's heart, if not in fact, the day of the dictator is over. The totalitarian era is passing, its old ideas blown away like leaves from an ancient, lifeless tree. A new breeze is blowing, and a nation refreshed by freedom stands ready to push on. There is new ground to be broken, and new action to be taken. There are times when the future seems thick as a fog; you sit and wait, hoping the mists will lift and reveal the right path. But this is a time when the future seems a door you can walk right through into a room called tomorrow.

(George H. Bush, 20 January 1989)

http://www.presidency.ucsb.edu/ws/index.php?pid=16610

6.8   Schemes: two-part contrasts

Whereas tropes make an idea salient through marked word choice exploiting denotation-connotation, euphemism-dysphemism and figures of speech, **schemes** amplify a message via marked two-part and three-part patterns. According to Max Atkinson (2004), the simplest way to frame information is through a two-part contrast (e.g. *good-bad, blessing-bane, cause-effect, problem-solutio*n). As Atkinson (2004) emphasises, many of the quotations we remember best employ this pattern, as illustrated by these examples from Atkinson (p.183):

It is more blessed to give than to receive. ***The Bible*** (Acts 20:35)

Live as if you were to die tomorrow.
Learn as if you were to live forever. **Mahatma Ghandi**

I stand here before you not as a prophet
but as a humble servant of you, the people. **Nelson Mandela**

All three quotations above contrast two things, but do so in different ways. The first example uses comparative contrast (*more this than that*). The second uses two sets of opposites — live vs. die and tomorrow vs. forever. And, the third employs a *not this but that* pattern of contradiction. This gives us three adaptable forms of contrast, which Atkinson (2004) labels:

❖ **Comparison**   *more this than that*

❖ **Opposition**   *this or that*

❖ **Contradiction**   *not this but that*

To make the contrast even more salient, rhetors can use a scheme that Atkinson (2004) dubs **phrase reversal** because a phrase is repeated in reverse. Literary scholars label this scheme **chiasmus** (from the Greek letter Chi χ because of the criss-cross pattern that results, as illustrated in the well-known quote by Winston Churchill below.

He who fails to plan

is planning to fail.

Another political rhetor who uses chiasmus in a variety of ways is former US President John F. Kennedy. In these two examples from his Presidential inauguration address on 20 January 1961 (full text available online), Kennedy embeds chiasmus within a **contradiction** pattern of contrast:

> *Ask not what your country can do for you;*
> *ask what you can do for your country,*

> *Let us never negotiate out of fear,*
> *but let us never fear to negotiate.*

In this next example from his address to the United Nations General Assembly on September 25, 1961 (full text available online), Kennedy embeds chiasmus in an **opposition** pattern of contrast:

> *Mankind must put an end to war,*
> *Or war will put an end to mankind.*

In section 5.7, I highlighted that coherence entails both matching and sequence clause relations. In the example below, Britain's war-time Prime Minister employs matching relations of compatibility and contrast by embedding the repeated clause *We shall fight* within a larger two-part contrast between fighting and surrendering. In spoken discourse, listeners typically get only one chance to catch an idea. So, rhetors can reinforce an idea by repeating it. Repetition also allows rhetors build rhythmically to a climax, as Winston Churchill does in this famous World War II speech to the House of Commons on June 4, 1940 (full text available online):

> *We shall fight on the beaches,*
> *we shall fight on the landing grounds,*
> *we shall fight in the fields and in the streets,*
> *we shall fight in the hills;*
> *we shall never surrender*

Compare Churchill's version with this paraphrase: *We shall fight on the beaches, the landing grounds, the fields and streets and hills.* This boring laundry list of locations fails to adequately convey the British resolve to fight, enacted by the repeated commissive *we shall fight* — what's constant is the will to fight; what varies is where they will fight. Churchill then amplifies this message through a two-part contrast: whereas the first four commissives emphasise what Britain will do (fight), the final commissive hammers home what they will never do (surrender).

Atkinson (2004) explains that two-part contrasts accentuate a message by creating a pattern of repetition, balance and anticipation. If you look back at all the examples of contrast discussed above, you'll notice that words or phrases from the first part are repeated in the second part. As a result, the two parts of the contrast are not just similar in length, but sound very similar, making it easier for the audience to spot what varies within a frame that remains constant. Further, two-part contrasts create anticipation by setting up a puzzle or question in the listener's mind. For example, if we are *not* supposed to ask what our country can do for us, then what *are* we supposed to ask? The first part of Kennedy's two-part contrast places the question in our mind; the second part provides the answer (*ask what you can do for your country*).

As in the Churchill example, two-part contrasts are often employed alongside repetition. In the excerpt below, Barack Obama uses the repeated directive *Look at Berlin* to frame the new information in each consecutive paragraph:

> *Look at Berlin*, where Germans and Americans learned to work together and trust each other less than three years after facing each other on the field of battle.

> *Look at Berlin*, where the determination of a people met the generosity of the Marshall Plan and created a German miracle; where a victory over tyranny gave rise to NATO, the greatest alliance ever formed to defend our common security.

Look at Berlin, where the bullet holes in the buildings and the somber stones and pillars near the Brandenburg Gate insist that we never forget our common humanity.

(Barack Obama, Berlin, 24 July 2008)
http://edition.cnn.com/2008/POLITICS/07/24/obama.words/
http://www.youtube.com/watch?v=Q-9ry38AhbU

In the excerpt below, another political rhetor uses repetition to frame new information and signal paragraph breaks. Listeners can't *see* paragraph breaks. So, speakers have to signal them, rhythmically and intonationally. By opening and closing each paragraph the same way, Ted Kennedy signals where each paragraph starts and ends. Notice, too, how each paragraph is framed around a single quote from the Republican nominee, whose identity is withheld until the end, creating a puzzle-solution effect:

The same Republicans who are talking about the crisis of unemployment *have nominated a man who once said, and I quote*, "Unemployment insurance is a prepaid vacation plan for freeloaders." *And that nominee is no friend of* labor.

The same Republicans who are talking about the problems of the inner cities *have nominated a man who said, and I quote*, "I have included in my morning and evening prayers every day the prayer that the Federal Government not bail out New York." *And that nominee is no friend of* this city and our great urban centers across this nation.

The same Republicans who are talking about security for the elderly *have nominated a man who said just four years ago that* "Participation in social security should be made voluntary." *And that nominee is no friend of* the senior citizens of this nation.

The same Republicans who are talking about preserving the environment *have nominated a man who last year made the preposterous statement, and I quote*, "Eighty percent of our air pollution comes from plants and trees." *And that nominee is no friend of* the environment.

And the same Republicans who are invoking Franklin Roosevelt *have nominated a man who said in 1976, and these are his exact words*, "Fascism was really the basis of the New Deal." *And that nominee whose name is Ronald Reagan has no right to* quote Franklin Delano Roosevelt.

(Ted Kennedy, Democratic National Convention, NY, 12 August 1980)
http://www.americanrhetoric.com/speeches/tedkennedy1980dnc.htm

Two-part contrasts create implicit puzzle-solution patterns, as we saw above. Rhetors can also create explicit **puzzle-solution patterns** by asking one or more questions. As Atkinson (2004) observes, even though audience members "know that they are not actually going to have to answer the speaker's question [out loud], it will still make them sit up and start wondering what's coming next" (p.192). In short, once a question has been posed, audiences will be listening closely for the answer. And, witty answers can enhance a rhetor's *ethos* because we tend to like smart, funny people.

Questions can also function as **transition devices**, signalling the rhetorical structure of a text, as illustrated below:

> *Thus far, I have been talking about the problem. So, what's the solution?*

> *So much for the past and the present. What about the future?*

A special kind of question used by rhetors is the **rhetorical question,** which unlike a genuine information-seeking question, is really a statement formulated as a question. When classical Roman rhetor Marcus Tullius Cicero asks *Of all nature's gifts to the human race, what is sweeter to a man than his children?* the answer he expects is *Nothing*. Similarly, when Abraham Lincoln asks the rhetorical question *What is conservatism? Is it not the adherence of the old and tried against the new and untried?* he clearly expects the audience to agree with him. As with any stylistic device, rhetorical questions need to be used judiciously. While supportive audiences may not mind rhetorical questions, hostile audiences may feel manipulated or backed into a corner.

6.9   Schemes: the rule of three

If the two-part contrast is the simplest way to accentuate a message, then the next most common rhetorical scheme is the rule of three. Like the two-part contrast, the rule of three projects salience through repetition, balance and anticipation. The realtor's mantra *Location! Location! Location!* employs the rule of three, using repetition for emphasis. The statement attributed to Caesar (*I came. I saw. I conquered*) also embodies the rule of three, but this time in a pattern of contrast in which the triumphalism of the final verb *conquered* contrasts with the mildness of the first two verbs (*came* and *saw*).

Once you start looking for the rule of three, you're likely to see it everywhere, in advertising slogans (*Beanz Meanz Heinz. Snap, Crackle, Pop*), in titles (*The Three Little Pigs, The Three Musketeers*), in morphological patterns (*good, better, best*), in the story structure of 'quest' narratives (departure, initiation, return), in the way we view time (past, present, future) and the way we categorise ideas (thesis, antithesis, synthesis).

As a rhetorical scheme, the rule of three can appear at the level of:

words	*faith, hope and charity*
phrases	*government of the people, by the people, for the people*
clauses	*Happiness is when what you think, what you say, and what you do are in harmony.*
sentences	*Dogs look up to us. Cats look down on us. Pigs treat us as equals.*

And, rhetors can combine the rule of three with other schemes like the two-part contrast and question-based puzzle-solution pattern, as illustrated in the excerpt below from former British Prime Minister Tony Blair's address to the Labour Party Conference in October 1996. Blair instantiates the Puzzle-Solution scheme by anticipating and voicing a question that the audience must surely be contemplating at this point: *What are your three main priorities for government Mr Blair?* The noun phrase *my three main priorities for government* creates an expectation that Blair will name three priorities. Instead, Blair offers one word *education* in a repeated rule of three to build to a lectern-thumping climax, thereby enacting and amplifying the importance of education in his agenda.

Question	*Ask me my three main priorities for government?*
Answer	*And I tell you*
Rule of Three	*education,* *education* *and education.*

Watch the clip at http://www.youtube.com/watch?v=2kAhChC_qxU

Here's another example of the bait-and-switch repetition-for-emphasis rule of three from American writer Henry James: *There are three things important in human life. The first is to be kind. The second is to be kind. The third is to be kind.* Are we left in any doubt as to what James considered important in human life?

Activity 6.10

US President Abraham Lincoln delivered his Gettysburg Address during the American Civil War, at the (makeshift) Soldier's National Cemetery in Gettysburg Pennsylvania, where the Union had won a decisive but costly battle just four months earlier. What is Lincoln's key message, and how do his stylistic choices, including rhetorical tropes and schemes, help to amplify his message? Answer clearly, concisely and coherently in 500 words or less.

Fourscore and seven years ago our fathers brought forth on this continent a new nation, conceived in liberty and dedicated to the proposition that all men are created equal.

Now we are engaged in a great civil war, testing whether that nation or any nation so conceived and so dedicated can long endure. We are met on a great battlefield of that war. We have come to dedicate a portion of that field as a final resting-place for those who here gave their lives that that nation might live. It is altogether fitting and proper that we should do this.

But, in a larger sense, we cannot dedicate, we cannot consecrate, we cannot hallow this ground. The brave men, living and dead who struggled here have consecrated it far above our poor power to add or detract. The world will little note nor long remember what we say here, but it can never forget what they did here. It is for us the living rather to be dedicated here to the unfinished work which they who fought here have thus far so nobly advanced. It is rather for us to be here dedicated to the great task remaining before us — that from these honored dead we take increased devotion to that cause for which they gave the last full measure of devotion — that we here highly resolve that these dead shall not have died in vain, that this nation under God shall have a new birth of freedom, and that government of the people, by the people, for the people shall not perish from the earth.

(Abraham Lincoln, 19 November 1863)

http://www.americanrhetoric.com/speeches/gettysburgaddress.htm

To learn more about the rule of three employed in political rhetoric, visit Max Atkinson's blog at http://maxatkinson.blogspot.com. Look also for video clips from the 27-minute television documentary *Claptrap: How to win a standing ovation* (1984) on YouTube.

In the next chapter, we review our learning journey so that you can customise your portable rhetorical toolkit for analysing persuasion messages wherever you may encounter them.

References

Atkinson, Max. (2004). *Lend Me Your Ears: All you need to know about making speeches and presentations*. London: Vermilion.

Beardsley, Monroe C. (1970). *The Possibility of Criticism*. Detroit: Wayne State University.

Booth, Wayne C. and Gregory, Marshall W. (1991). *The Harper & Row rhetoric: Writing as thinking and thinking as writing* (2nd edition) New York: HarperCollins.

Hymes, Dell. (1972). Models of the interaction of language and social life. In J. Gumperz and D. Hymes (Eds.), *Directions in Sociolinguistics: The Ethnography of Communication.* New York: Holt, Rinehart & Winston, pp.35-71.

Lanham, Richard A. (2003). *Analyzing Prose* (2nd edition) London: Continuum.

Lutz, William. (1996). *The New Doublespeak: Why no one knows what anyone's saying anymore.* HarperCollins.

Mauk, John. (2006). *Inventing Arguments*. Boston: Wadsworth.

Selzer, Jack. (2004). Rhetorical Analysis: Understanding how texts persuade readers. In Charles Bazerman & Paul Prior (eds.) *What writing does and how it does it: An introduction to analyzing texts and textual practices.* New Jersey: Lawrence Erlbaum, pp. 279-307.

Weaver, Richard M. 1953. Ultimate Terms in Contemporary Rhetoric. *The Ethics of Rhetoric.* Chicago: H. Regnery, pp. 212-32.

Chapter 7 The big picture

What must I remember when...

❖ selecting an analytical framework?

❖ inferring communicative purpose?

❖ identifying the audience?

❖ analysing ethos?

7.1   Selecting an analytical framework

Our exploration of argument design is rooted in Aristotle's canons of invention, organisation and style, informed by the work of applied linguists, anthropologists, psychologists, philosophers, and literary scholars. My aim has been to synthesise ideas so you could customise for yourself a portable rhetorical toolkit for analysing arguments in a linguistically-informed manner.

You could, for instance, use Hymes's (1972) SPEAKING mnemonic (see Figure 2.4). Alternatively, you could use the analytical lexicon (see Figure 7.1) developed by rhetoricians Karlyn Campbell and Susan Huxman, highlighting seven key elements of rhetorical action:

1. **Purpose**: the conclusion argued (thesis) and the response desired by the rhetor. Some purposes are *instrumental*; they seek overt action from the audience. Some purposes are *consummatory*; they seek appreciation, contemplation, or conferring honor or blame.

2. **Audience**: the receivers of a rhetorical act. This includes an immediate audience, a target audience, and a role created by the rhetor for the audience, or specialized audiences (VIPs) with social or political power to effect change.

3. **Persona**: the role(s) adopted by the persuader in making the argument (e.g., teacher, preacher, reporter, prophet, mediator, and the like)

4. **Tone**: the rhetor's attitude toward the subject (detached, emotional, satirical, and so forth) and towards the audience (personal/ impersonal, authoritative/ egalitarian/ supplicant, and so on).

5. **Evidence**: the different kinds of support material for the argument.

6. **Structure**: the way the materials are organized to gain attention, develop a case, and provide emphasis.

7. **Strategies**: the adaptation of all the above, including language, appeals, and argument, to shape the materials to overcome the challenges the rhetor faces (the rhetorical context).

(Campbell & Huxman, 2009, p.24)

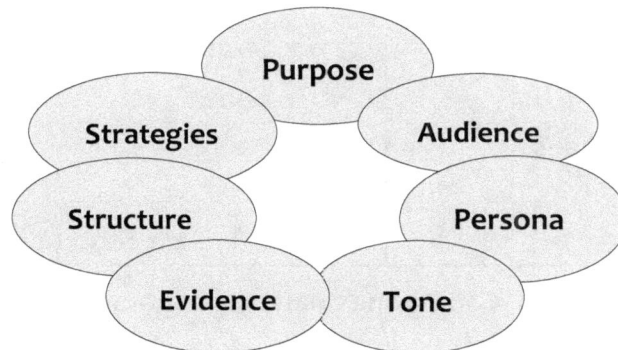

Figure 7.1 **Campbell and Huxman's (2009, p.25) analytical lexicon**

Both Hymes's (1972) SPEAKING mnemonic and Campbell and Huxman's (2009) lexicon represent heuristics to be applied thoughtfully (not checklists to be mindlessly ticked off). As I emphasised in chapter 1, the purpose of a linguistic analysis is not to evaluate the effectiveness of a text but to explain how it works. When beginning an analysis, it's important to have a clear purpose — a question (puzzle) that your analysis is meant to answer (solve). Campbell and Huxman's (2009, p.26) analysis of US President Abraham Lincoln's Gettysburg Address, for instance, seeks to answer three WH-questions (Why has this speech lived on as a rhetorical force? What does the speech reveal about Lincoln's rhetorical artistry? How can words contribute to the making of history?)

I would suggest that it's wiser to answer ONE question rigorously than a bunch of questions superficially. A linguistic analysis, after all, is an argument about how a text works. Two rhetorical analysts working on the same text could generate different analyses. So, it's incumbent on all analysts to demonstrate that their analysis:

(1) answers a question that a jury of their peers (fellow analysts) consider worthwhile.

(2) follows the evidence, neither omitting crucial (textual and contextual) clues nor distorting meaning.

(3) adheres to Occam's Razor, or the Law of Parsimony which states *Among competing hypotheses, select the one that makes the fewest assumptions, thereby offering the simplest explanation of the effect observed.* (NB: simple ≠ simplistic)

In short, a convincing linguistic analysis proposes an explanation of how a text works by engaging in *elenkhos* (see section 5.4), anticipating and responding to alternative interpretations.

If we compare Campbell and Huxman's (2009) lexicon with Hymes's (1972) SPEAKING mnemonic, you'll notice the overlaps in the two frameworks (see Figure 7.2).

Hymes's SPEAKING mnemonic	Campbell and Huxman's lexicon
Situation (*setting, scene*)	
Participants	Audience, Persona
Ends	Purpose
Acts	Strategies
Key	Tone
Instrumentalities	
Norms	
Genre	Evidence, Structure

Figure 7.2   Comparing analytical frameworks

At the end of the day, it's up to you to select or synthesise a framework best suited to the analytical task at hand. And, as you begin your analysis, start by identifying the communicative purpose of the text(s) under scrutiny. As mentioned at the outset of our journey, discourse is a form of social action. Language use is never random, but serves ideational and social purposes simultaneously. As speech act theory recognises, *saying is doing*, and all utterances have an underlying intent (what the speaker means), which can be expressed overtly through direct speech acts or covertly through indirect speech acts (see sections 3.8 and 3.9).

7.2   Inferring communicative purpose

As applied linguist John Swales (1990) emphasises, genres emerge in response to recurrent communicative needs, and are thus best identified in terms of the communicative purpose(s) they're meant to serve. Aristotle's three genres of rhetoric (forensic, epideictic and deliberative) each map onto a specific communicative purpose (see sections 2.7 and 4.2). So, as an analyst, your first task is to identify the genre of the persuasion message under scrutiny via rhetorical purpose. Is the text's purpose to establish the truth, to judge value or to decide policy (see Figure 7.3)?

Genre of rhetoric	Argument type	Communicative Purpose
Forensic	Empirical	Establish or refute that X is the case
	Definitional	Establish or refute that X is Y
Epideictic	Value	Praise X as good
		Villify X as bad
Deliberative	Policy	Exhort the audience to do X
		Dissuade the audience from doing X

Figure 7.3   Identifying communicative purpose

Identifying communicative purpose is straightforward, if the rhetor states it, e.g. *My name is Harvey Milk, and I'm here to recruit you*. But, rhetors don't always state their communicative purpose, leaving audiences and analysts in the shared position of having to infer the rhetor's purpose from textual and contextual clues (see Figure 2.1).

A good place to start this inferential work is to ask what occasioned the persuasion message, since all rhetoric is a response to a situation or (chain of) event(s) that somebody frames as requiring a timely response. Timeliness is of utmost importance in persuasion messages because we're all familiar with the adage *Too little, too late*. The ancient Greeks had two words for time: *chronos* (meaning sequential time, from which we get the English word *chronological*) and *kairos* (referring to the appropriate time to seize an opportunity). Classical rhetors understood that they had to frame situations as ripe for response, anticipating the audience's question *Why are you raising this issue NOW?*

Let's clarify **kairos** with an example. On November, 19, 1863, US President Abraham Lincoln made a speech at the battlefield of Gettysburg, Pennsylvania, where the Union had won an important but costly battle just four months earlier. The American Civil War was still raging, and a depleted and exhausted citizenry was beginning to doubt the wisdom of the entire enterprise. Lincoln was at Gettysburg to consecrate the makeshift cemetery and eulogise the war dead (see Activity 6.10 for the full text of Lincoln's speech). At less than 300 words, Lincoln's speech is a masterpiece of conciseness. But, part of the reason the Gettysburg Address is considered one of the greatest short speeches in American history is that Lincoln took the eulogy genre, an example of epideictic rhetoric associated with flowery phrases and ornamental speech, and transformed it into a clarion call to action.

The process begins with Lincoln's masterful use of *kairos*. Did you notice, for instance, that Lincoln starts his speech with neither the Civil War in general, the battle of Gettysburg in particular, nor even the dedication ceremony that he was there to officiate? These, he introduces in crisp, clear phrases in the second paragraph, reserving the prime location of his opening for a look back at America's constitutional history (*Fourscore and seven years ago our fathers brought forth on this continent a new nation, conceived in liberty and dedicated to the proposition that all men are created equal*) to remind his audience of what's at stake — not just their personal freedoms but the very life of the nation.

The story that Lincoln chooses to tell begins not with death, the literal reason for the Gettysburg assembly, but with its opposite, the birth of *a new nation, conceived in liberty* (notice Lincoln's explicit use of positive values like *new* and *liberty*; see section 4.6). Lincoln paints with words, combining metaphor and two-part contrast to frame the fallen soldiers, not against the background of the grim battlefield where they lost their lives, but against the founding principles of the nation they died fighting for.

Lincoln then advocates the best way to honour the war dead — to finish the work they began (*It is for us the living, rather, to be dedicated here to the unfinished work which they who fought here have thus far so nobly advanced*). Lincoln's closing words build to a climax as he states his desired response (*that we here highly resolve that these dead shall not have died in vain...*). Eulogies serve to memorialise the dead, and Lincoln could have framed his Gettysburg Address around the terrible death toll on the battlefield. Instead, he *changes the frame* to *change the game* (see section 4.7) shifting the focus of the gathered populace from death to birth, from desolation to renewed hope and a shared resolve to protect democracy.

Kairos underscores the importance of **framing effects** (see the tropes and schemes discussed in chapter 6) to bend people's hearts and minds towards a desired conception of reality. So, *kairos* is a good place to start in terms of inferring a rhetor's communicative purpose. A second strand of evidence we can use to identify a text's communicative purpose is the arguer's main claim. As summarised in Figure 7.2, the four types of issues or questions (empirical, definitional, value and policy) each map onto a specific rhetorical purpose.

Attending to *kairos* and identifying the rhetor's main claim represent two means for inferring the rhetor's communicative purpose. When interpreting any text, it's always a good idea to use multiple sources of evidence, or what researchers dub the method of triangulation or independent corroboration. The assumption here is that an interpretation is more likely to be reliable, the more strands of evidence which point towards it. So, the more textual and contextual clues we use, and the more these different clues dovetail, or converge towards an interpretation, the more confident we can be that we haven't distorted the text. Conversely, if the evidence seems uncertain or equivocal, we need to be appropriately cautious, qualifying our statements so as not to overstate the case.

7.3   Analysing the audience

In section 3.2, we classified arguments into dyadic and triadic, based on who the decision-maker is: the arguers themselves or a third-party audience. In **dyadic arguments**, arguers address one another, and decide whether and how far to assent to each other's arguments. In **triadic arguments**, arguers address a third-party audience, who decides which argument is more compelling.

Audience analysis begins with identifying the audience as precisely as possible. As discussed in section 6.1, identity is relational, and rhetors enact a **persona** by harnessing a particular style to construct a text-world relationship with their audience. For instance, by performing a formal impersonal style, rhetors can project detachment and hierarchy. In contrast, by performing an informal personal style, arguers can create **synthetic intimacy**, drawing the audience into a close peer-to-peer text-world relationship.

As emphasised throughout this volume, discourse is a design tool that we use both to mirror and shape reality. So, when analysing any text, it's important to distinguish between our real-world relationships (as employers, employees, parents, children, siblings, spouses or friends) and the text-world relationships we construct by performing different personas through our stylistic choices (see section 3.6). The **real-world audience** is the physical audience whom the rhetor addresses, identifiable in terms of demographic details like age, sex, sexual orientation, educational level, socioeconomic status, and political and religious affiliations (see section 3.4). This audience can comprise one person as in a personal letter or a multitude of people. Obviously, the larger the audience, the greater the odds of its being mixed or heterogeneous, in terms of knowledge, interest and support for the issue and rhetor (see Figures 3.5, 3.8 and 5.5). As Mills (2000) suggests, rhetors faced with mixed audiences may need to group them into primary, secondary and tertiary audiences in order to decide whose needs to address first (see section 4.5). A classic example of a public address in which a political rhetor addresses several audiences in a sequential manner is US President Ronald Reagan's televised address, delivered on 28 January 1986, in response to the *Challenger* space shuttle tragedy.

Activity 7.1

Listen to US President Ronald Reagan's televised address, delivered on 28 January 1986, in response to the *Challenger* space shuttle tragedy. You can view the four- minute address on YouTube by keying in the words *challenger address ronald reagan*. Write a 500-word analysis, identifying the various audiences that Reagan addresses and why Reagan addresses them in the order that he does, keeping in mind Reagan's rhetorical purpose and genre norms.

Whereas the real-world audience comprises the physical audience addressed by a rhetor, the **text-world audience** is an imagined audience invoked by the rhetor through stylistic cues which cast the audience in a particular rhetorical role for the duration of the persuasion message. Among the first to discuss the two audiences was literary scholar Walker Gibson (1950) who distinguishes between an actual "armchair" audience and a purely textual "mock" audience (pp.265-266). Rhetorician Wayne Booth (1961) refers to the text-world reader as the "implied reader" (p.138). John Preston (1970) uses the label "created reader" (p.2), while Arthur Sherbo (1969) uses the label "inside reader" to contrast with "outside reader" (p.36). More recently, Lisa Ede and Andrea Lunsford (1984) have used the labels "audience addressed" and "audience invoked" (p.156) to distinguish between real-world and text-world audiences.

Not surprisingly, most of the research on interior/exterior, real/fictional, or addressed/invoked audiences relates to written texts, given that writers and readers are not usually co-present, and often don't know one another. Yet, writers can create the fiction of a close egalitarian relationship by performing an informal personal style. Alternatively, they can select a more formal impersonal style to project a more hierarchical and distant relationship. In short, the stylistic resources of language allow rhetors to construct the kind of ideal relationship they envisage with their audience.

When analysing a rhetor's style, we attend to the rhetor's voice and tonal choices. As Booth and Marshall (1991) explain, voice refers to the persona or character role that the rhetor adopts over the entire length of the text, whereas tone refers to the rhetor's attitude to subject matter and audience. Recall the analogy they use of the human face: voice is to a rhetor's identity as face is to one's identity, and tone corresponds to the myriad transitory expressions (fear, disgust, sorrow, anger, etc.) that flit across a person's face (see section 6.1).

Dell Hymes (1972) uses the term *key* rather than tone in his SPEAKING mnemonic because he, too, was thinking figuratively, only his analogy is drawn from music and alludes to the emotional resonances created by different musical keys. Just as a song composed in a major key feels happy and upbeat while that composed in a minor key feels plangent or sorrowful, so also a rhetor's tonal choices reflect different attitudes towards the audience and the subject matter being discussed. Note, for instance, the solemn tone that Lincoln adopts in his Gettysburg Address (*We have come to dedicate a portion of that field, as a final resting place for those who here gave their lives that this nation might live. It is altogether fitting that we should do this*).

As discussed in section 3.6, the voice, or persona that a rhetor adopts affects his or her *ethos* — the audience's perception of the rhetor's trustworthiness as a person of good will, good sense and good character, based on WHAT is said and HOW it is said. *Ethos* captures the idea that rhetors must not only be trustworthy but must be perceived to be trustworthy. And, the voice or persona which the rhetor adopts has a significant impact on this perception.

7.4　Analysing *ethos*

Michael Leff (2003) analyses *ethos* in terms of the elements of rhetorical embodiment, rhetorical enactment, and rhetorical evocation, illustrating his method through a close reading of Martin Luther King Jr.'s (1963) "Letter from Birmingham Jail". King's letter was written in response to a chain of events spanning a week in April 1963. On 10 April, the city government of Birmingham, Alabama, passed a legal provision banning street marches. On 12 April, King was arrested and placed in solitary confinement in Birmingham Jail for participating in peaceful demonstrations against segregation. On the same day, eight white Alabama clergymen issued the open letter "A call for unity" in a local newspaper, criticising King and the Birmingham movement for inciting civil disturbances. King's letter, written in long hand, in his jail cell, is a response to this public statement, as the opening sentences of his letter make clear. The full text of King's Letter and the Alabama clergymen's statement are available online. Read both so that you can compare your reading of King's "Letter" with Michael Leff's.

Leff's notion of *ethos* draws on Alan Brinton's (1985) observation that the rhetor needs to be "someone we can trust to express our shared values, to think in terms of our common assumptions, to exercise good judgment, and to speak for us" (p.55). To do this, Leff (2003) argues, rhetors need to embody the *ethos* (character) of the society they are addressing. Such **rhetorical embodiment** is especially important in deliberative rhetoric, which advocates actions based on values of benefit and harm, honour and expedience, which, like all values, are societally and culturally influenced. Leff (2003) highlights two main ways in which Martin Luther King Jr. embodies the *ethos* of his 1963 American audience, in his "Letter from Birmingham Jail":

❖ **direct statements** to associate himself with the basic American principles of democracy, equality and liberty and to endorse the American dream as construed in the Constitution and Declaration of Independence.

❖ **allusions to authoritative figures** from American history (the Founding Fathers, Abraham Lincoln and Thomas Jefferson) as well as the Judeo-Christian and Western intellectual traditions (e.g. the Apostle Paul, the prophet Amos, Jesus, St Augustine, St Thomas Aquinas, Socrates, Reinhold Niebuhr, Martin Luther, Martin Buber, John Bunyan, Paul Tillich and T.S. Eliot).

Whether through verbatim quotation or allusion, **rhetorical embodiment** involves borrowing the language and style of respected figures, thereby achieving trust by association (*the friend of my friend is also my friend*). Leff (2003) suggests that King appeals to these authorities to vindicate and explain his own actions. For example, King responds to the charge of being an outsider (literally and ideologically) by showing that his views do NOT depart from respectable American opinion. King cites Scriptural precedent as well as icons of belief and faith accepted by his American audience, such as St Paul, Amos, Jesus, Socrates, St Augustine, Martin Luther and Martin Buber, to persuade his readers that agitation in the cause of overcoming injustice is not a threat to the common tradition, but rather a way of renewing and sustaining its energy.

Rhetorical enactment in turn involves dramatising one's message for maximum experiential impact. It responds to the audience's cry, *Show me! Don't just tell me!* by ensuring that style and substance reinforce each other. To accentuate a message, rhetors harness tropes and schemes (see sections 6.5 to 6.9) to amplify WHAT is being said by HOW it is said.

To illustrate rhetorical enactment in King's "Letter", Leff (2003) highlights the restrained energy and balanced judgment that King enacts in response to the Alabama clergymen's accusation that King is a radical, lacking good judgment and acting without due regard for consequences. As Leff points out, this enactment occurs through a pattern in which King responds to the allegations against him on two levels: an immediate practical level followed by a level of higher-order principles.

In terms of its overall shape, King's "Letter" is constructed as a series of refutations of seven claims, which King attributes to the clergymen he's responding to. The first of these refutations provides a clear example of the dual pattern of progression highlighted by Leff (2003). In response to the charge of being an outsider, King offers an immediate practical explanation for his presence in Birmingham — the Birmingham affiliate of the Southern Christian Leadership Conference asked for his assistance; so, King is "here along with several members of my staff, because we were invited here".

King immediately follows this practical explanation up with the larger moral imperative that has led him to Alabama: "But more basically, I am in Birmingham because injustice is here". Arguing by precedent, using the Bible as his source, King explains that just as the Old Testament prophets of the eighth century BC and the Apostle Paul left their villages to carry God's word far beyond their home towns, King too is "compelled to carry the gospel of freedom beyond [his] own home town".

To place the issue against an even broader backdrop, King moves from a biblical to a secular perspective, highlighting "the interrelatedness of all countries and states" such that "injustice anywhere is a threat to justice everywhere". Leff (2003) suggests that as this pattern unfolds, the reader witnesses King exercising the kind of judgment most appropriate to deliberative rhetoric, namely, judgment that encompasses both particulars and principles, questions of honour and of expediency.

According to Leff, the most notable example of rhetorical enactment in King's "Letter", is King's carefully modulated response to the charge that the demonstrations were untimely. King begins this segment of his text by reminding his readers that African Americans have already been waiting 340 years for their rights. What follows is a 316-word sentence, the longest in the letter, which rhetorically enacts the Negro's experience of waiting.

King harnesses the resources of English syntax, combining two patterns. First, he uses a left-branching sentence structure in which the dependent clause precedes the main clause. Second, he piles on ten dependent clauses, functioning as Adjuncts of time, all of which start the same way, "when you..." (see bolded text in quote below). What varies within this constant frame is the action performed in each clause.

This combination of patterns allows King to effectively suspend completion of the sentence. Readers have no choice but to wait till the end of the mounting accretion of clauses to arrive at the closure provided by the main clause. Through its marked structure and length, the sentence rhetorically **enacts** the Negro's experience of waiting as no propositional argument ever could:

> **But when you** have seen vicious mobs lynch your mothers and fathers at will and drown your sisters and brothers at whim; **when you** have seen hate filled policemen curse, kick and even kill your black brothers and sisters; **when you** see the vast majority of your twenty million Negro brothers smothering in an airtight cage of poverty in the midst of an affluent society; **when you** suddenly find your tongue twisted and your speech stammering as you seek to explain to your six year old daughter why she can't go to the public amusement park that has just been advertised on television, and see tears welling up in her eyes when she is told that Funtown is closed to colored children, and see ominous clouds of inferiority beginning to form in her little mental sky, and see her beginning to distort her personality by developing an unconscious bitterness toward white people; **when you** have to concoct an answer for a five year old son who is asking: "Daddy, why do white people treat colored people so mean?"; **when you** take a cross-country drive and find it necessary to sleep night after night in the

uncomfortable corners of your automobile because no motel will accept you; **when you** are humiliated day in and day out by nagging signs reading "white" and "colored"; **when your** first name becomes "nigger," your middle name becomes "boy" (however old you are) and your last name becomes "John," and your wife and mother are never given the respected title "Mrs."; **when you** are harried by day and haunted by night by the fact that you are a Negro, living constantly at tiptoe stance, never quite knowing what to expect next, and are plagued with inner fears and outer resentments; **when you** are forever fighting a degenerating sense of "nobodiness"— then you will understand why we find it difficult to wait.

(Martin Luther King Jr., 1963, emphasis mine)

The sentence is also marked by its surprising ending. Given the mounting tension of the cumulative images portraying the effects of bigotry, we might have expected the sentence to climax in outrage against those asking King and his people to continue to wait. Instead of vitriol, however, we get the calmly-worded main clause "Then you will understand why we find it difficult to wait". As Leff (2003) remarks, the understatement not only amplifies the emotional impact but enacts King's restraint, his pledge to proceed reasonably and patiently.

To summarise the discussion thus far, **rhetorical embodiment** refers to rhetors' embodiment of societal values (see section 4.6) through direct statements and/or allusions to authoritative figures and respected source texts. **Rhetorical enactment** in turn involves harnessing tropes and schemes to dramatise the persuasion message for maximum experiential impact.

Rhetorical evocation in turn entails evoking a suitable persona to reframe reality as the rhetor desires. In deliberative rhetoric, for example, rhetors typically frame problems as arising out of a misalignment between belief and conduct. When an audience accepts certain principles but fails to act on them, the rhetor's delicate and difficult task is to help the audience acknowledge this inconsistency.

According to Leff (2003), King evokes a prophetic persona in order to reframe the Alabama clergymen's depiction of King as an outsider. The point, as Leff observes, is that prophets are members of the tribe, who criticise a society from within, incarnating what is highest and best in that society in order to summon their people to act on these ideals. The white Alabama clergymen also paint King as an impatient black man. King could have chosen a 'divide and conquer' *Us against Them* approach in response. Instead, he reframes the divisive *Black against White* situation by reinterpreting old, shared icons to create a new vision for 1960s America. The prophet seeks to lead his people to higher ground, and that is the relationship with his audience which King rhetorically evokes in his "Letter".

Activity 7.2

Analyse Lincoln's *ethos* in the Gettysburg Address in terms of Leff's (2003)

❖ **rhetorical embodiment,** in which the rhetor embodies the audience's social values through explicit and/or implicit reference(s) to shared icons, authoritative figures and respected source texts.

❖ **rhetorical enactment,** in which the rhetor dramatises his/her message using tropes and schemes that amplify its experiential impact.

❖ **rhetorical evocation,** in which the rhetor evokes a suitable persona to reframe things in the way s/he desires

Activity 7.3

How is *ethos* to be enacted in Volkswagen ads? Answer in 300 words or less.

How to do a Volkswagen ad

1. Look at the car.

2. Look harder. You'll find enough advantages to fill a lot of ads. Like the air-cooled engine, the economy, the design that never goes out of date.

3. Don't exaggerate. For instance, some people have gotten 50 mpg and more from a VW. But others have only managed 28. Average: 32. Don't promise more.

4. Call a spade a spade. And a suspension a suspension. Not something like orbital cushioning.

5. Speak to the reader. Don't shout. He can hear you. Especially if you talk sense.

7.5   Analysing framing effects

In chapter 6, we explored style as a means of framing information to direct attention to some aspects of reality, while suppressing other aspects, resulting in a cueing, or **framing effect**. Which option (a) or (b) would you select to complete the sentence below?

> *We need to stop for petrol. The petrol tank is half _____.*

> (a) *full*   (b) *empty*

The old joke about optimists seeing the doughnut, pessimists, the hole, and realists, the whole, is a joke about framing effects — a topic that has attracted researchers from linguistics, social psychology (in particular, behavioural decision making), health psychology, communication, marketing, economics and politics. Simply put, *framing* refers to an addresser, often with a persuasion agenda, selecting one among many possible ways of presenting information. For example, I could describe a cut of meat as *25% fat* or *75% lean*. Logically, both propositions are equivalent. Rhetorically, however, the latter sounds better, especially to health-conscious consumers, given its emphasis on *lean*.

Framing can be value-neutral or value-laden. The term used for value-laden framing is **valence framing**, using a frame to cast information in an advantageous or disadvantageous light, accentuating the positive or the negative, respectively. In their discussion of **valence framing effects**, social psychologists Irwin Levin, Sandra Schneider and Gary Gath (1998) distinguish between three types of frames that language users can use:

❖ *Attribute framing*: where a specific attribute is described using positive terms or the corresponding negative terms, e.g. describing a cut of meat as 25% fat or 75% lean.

❖ *Risky choice framing*: where the options offered are associated with different risk levels, e.g. a sure option vs. an uncertain, and thus risky, option.

❖ *Goal framing*: where actions and situations are framed in terms of the positive consequences of attaining a goal (e.g. *performing self-breast examination may lead to early detection of potential cancer and consequently to higher chance of cure*) or the negative consequences of not attaining it (*not performing self-breast examination may lead to failure of early detection and decrease the chance of possible cure*).

Levin, Schneider and Gath's (1998) classification of frames is based on three parameters: what is framed, what is affected, and how the effect is measured, as summarised in Figure 7.4.

Frame type	What is framed	What is affected	How effect is measured
Risky choice	Set of options with different risk levels	Risk preference	Comparison of choices for risky options
Attribute	Object/event attributes or characteristics	Item evaluation	Comparison of attractiveness ratings for the single item
Goal	Consequence or implied goal of behavior	Impact of persuasion	Comparison of rate of adoption of the behavior

Figure 7.4 **Risky choice, attribute and goal framing (Levin *et al.*, 1998)**

Social psychologist Jerome Bruner (1957) defines perception as an act of categorisation, which answers the question *What am I looking at?* In other words, frames provide cues to infer the identity of a perceived object or event, and different categories imply different reference points for description and evaluation.

For example, in his experimental study, 'How to show that 9>221: Collect Judgments in a Between-Subjects Design', psychologist Michael Birnbaum (1999) asked one group of participants to judge *How large is the number 9?* and another group of participants to judge *How large is the number 221?* As the title of Birnbaum's paper suggests, the number 9 was judged to be larger than the number 221. Birnbaum explains this strange result in terms of the different frames against which each number was probably judged. Birnbaum speculates that the number 9 was most likely assessed in relation to one-digit numbers, where the lowest and highest reference points are 0 and 9, making 9 seem relatively large. In contrast, the number 221 was probably assessed in relation to three-digit numbers, where the lowest and highest reference points are 0 and 999, making 221 seem relatively small. Birnbaum ends by highlighting that if both groups were asked *Which is larger, 9 or 221?*, the unanimous answer would be 221, given the new frame comprising the reference points 9 and 221.

Activity 7.4

Given the two options presented in (a), which would you choose?
(a) *$500 now or $620 in 20 days*

Given the two options presented in (b), which would you choose?
(b) *$500 right now and $0 in 20 days OR $0 now and $620 in 20 days*

Did your answer change from presentation (a) to (b)? If it did, we can explain it, using Marc van Buiten and Gideon Keren's (2009) distinction between *separate presentation* and *joint presentation* of frames. *Joint presentation of frames* involves presenting both sides of a story, whereas *separate presentation of frames* involves selecting just one side to tell. Presentation (a) provides just one side of the story. The *$500 now* option focuses entirely on the present, while the *$620 in 20 days* option focuses entirely on the future, creating an *either-or* dichotomy, likely to cue a knee-jerk instant gratification outcome (*I'll take the $500 now. Thank you! Who knows what could happen in 20 days?*)

In contrast, presentation (b) slows things down with a *joint presentation of frames*, which shows both present and future consequences of each option — choosing $500 now means $0 in 20 days, whereas choosing $0 now means $620 in 20 days. Unlike presentation (a) which leaves the $0 consequences unattended to, presentation (b) makes salient all four data points, as shown below:

Separate presentation of frames		Joint presentation of frames	
NOW	**IN 20 DAYS**	**NOW**	**IN 20 DAYS**
$500	$620	$500	$0
		$0	$620

Changing the frame changes our internal representation of the choice options, and thus affects the choices we make. If I use *separate presentation of frames* to describe a cut of meat, e.g. *This cut of meat is 75% lean,* the reference point activated will likely be mono-dimensional: 0% to 100% lean. In contrast, if I describe the same cut of meat using *joint presentation of frames* (*This cut of meat is 75% lean and 25% fat*), I activate a comparative reference point, namely, the ratio of lean meat to fat.

According to van Buiten and Keren (2009), this distinction between *processing frames jointly* (being exposed simultaneously to both frames) and *processing frames separately* (being exposed to one or other, but not both frames) affects addressers and audiences, asymmetrically. To explore this asymmetry between addresser and audience, van Buiten and Keren (2009) used the *Asian disease* problem devised by Nobel Prize winners Amos Tversky and Daniel Kahneman (1981):

Tversky and Kahneman's (1981) Experimental condition 1

Imagine that the USA is preparing for an outbreak of an unusual Asian disease, which is expected to kill 600 people. Two alternative programs to combat the disease have been proposed. Assume that the exact scientific estimates of the consequences are as follows:

If Program A is adopted, 200 people will be saved.

If Program B is adopted, there is a 1/3 probability that 600 people will be saved and a 2/3 probability that no people will be saved.

Which of the two programs would you favour?

Tversky and Kahneman's (1981) Experimental condition 2

Imagine that the USA is preparing for an outbreak of an unusual Asian disease, which is expected to kill 600 people. Two alternative programs to combat the disease have been proposed. Assume that the exact scientific estimates of the consequences are as follows:

If Program C is adopted, 400 people will die.

If Program D is adopted, there is a 1/3 probability that nobody will die and a 2/3 probability that 600 people will die.

Which of the two programs would you favour?

Participants in van Buiten and Keren's (2009) experiments were exposed to the Sure and Risky programs, each stated in a positive (*lives saved*) and a negative (*people dying*) valence frame. Half the participants were asked to assume that they preferred the Sure program; the other half were asked to assume that they preferred the Risky program. Participants were then asked to choose which frame (positive or negative) they would use to convince the city council of their preference. Van Buiten and Keren (2009) found a high level of agreement between speakers and listeners in terms of a preference for the positive frame, when it came to the Sure program. As Figure 7.5 shows, most (76%) speakers promoting the Sure program chose the positive rather than negative frame. And, most (72%) listeners presented with a positive frame preferred the Sure program over the Risky program.

Valence Frame	Program type	Preferred choice of	
		Speakers	Listeners
positive	A: Sure, 200 will be saved	76%	72%
	B: Risky, p = 1/3 for 200 saved	84%	28%
negative	C: Sure, 400 will die	24%	22%
	D: Risky, p = 2/3 for 400 dead	16%	78%

Figure 7.5   Results of van Buiten and Keren's (2009) study

This symmetry did not, however, hold for the Risky program. Most (84%) speakers promoting the Risky program chose the positive rather than negative frame, suggesting speaker bias towards positive frames, generally. But, only 28% of listeners presented with a positive frame preferred the Risky program. Given this mismatch between speakers' and listeners' preferences, van Buiten and Keren (2009) conclude that speakers' choice of the positive frame for the Risky program may not be optimal, and that speakers would have been wiser to use the negative frame to promote the Risky program.

Activity 7.5

Is it safe to generalise from van Buiten and Keren's (2009) study that rhetors should always adopt a negative frame when recommending risky programs — why (not)?

One question that arises at this point is the extent to which framing effects occur automatically (without our awareness). Gail Fairhurst (2005), for example, suggests that some framing effects may simply be a result of priming, analogous to viewing the world through sunglasses, "one has the initial experience of less glare, but quickly forgets seeing through a colored lens. Our conscious experience has dissolved but primed our unconscious with a lens that influences our view, though we may be unaware of its presence" (p.169).

This leads to the question of whether or not framing is a teachable skill. When audiences are presented with a particular frame, do they automatically stick to the given frame? For instance, if an audience were told *400 out of 600 people will die*, would this frame block them from considering the complementary frame *200 out of the 600 people will live*?

Similarly, we don't know whether rhetors automatically consider more than one frame, when designing their persuasion messages. It may be that the context in which a message is uttered automatically determines the frame. If framing is mainly an automatic process, then training would entail teaching people how to suppress the first frame that springs to mind so that they can switch to deliberate consideration of alternative frames.

What we do know is that if addressers wish to remain neutral, they should use a *joint presentation of frames*. By presenting both frames simultaneously, rhetors would in effect be reducing bias by providing both sides (positive and negative) of the story. But, we would still be faced with a challenge, deciding which frame to put first/last, given the information value of sequencing. Putting good news before bad news would have a different impact to reversing the order. There's also the problem that from the perspective of Grice's maxims (see Figure 5.4), a joint presentation of frames may be perceived as redundant, failing to adhere to Grice's maxim of quantity (see Activity 7.6).

Activity 7.6

Do these utterances seem odd to you — why (not)?

(1) *This program will result in 200 people saved out of 600, i.e. 400 people dying.*

(2) *This task is 60% complete, that is, 40% still to be done.*

Activity 7.7

Develop a coherent analysis of the text below, paying attention to any ONE aspect (invention, organisation or style) that interests you.

How can rhyme make your influence climb?

P1   Is Gillette really the best a man can get? Are loose lips responsible for sinking ships? Is it true that the best part of waking up is Folgers in your cup? When it comes to seat belts, will I really get a ticket if I don't click it? And finally, compared to its competitors, is Bounty truly the quilted, thicker, quicker, picker-upper?

P2   From advertising to public service announcements, rhyming slogans are everywhere. Out of all the potential marketing strategies to choose from, why do so many organizations convey their message with rhymes? Part of it is that rhyming messages are more memorable and easily repeated to others, which should come as no surprise. But could it also be that rhyming statements are actually seen as more accurate and truthful?

P3   Noting the pervasiveness of rhyming proverbs such as "Birds of a feather flock together," social scientists Matthew McGlone and Jessica Tofighbaksh set out to investigate whether statements that rhyme are thought to be more accurate than those that don't. As part of their study, they took a number of rhyming sayings previously unknown to the study participants and created parallel but nonrhyming versions of them. For example they took the relatively obscure saying, "Caution and measure will win you treasure," and modified it to say, "Caution and measure will win you riches." As another example they took the saying, "What sobriety conceals, alcohol reveals," and changed it to "What sobriety conceals, alcohol unmasks."

P4   Participants then read some of these sayings and rated each one for the extent to which it accurately reflects the way the world really works. The researchers found that even though the participants in the study strongly held the belief that rhyming was in no way an indicator of accuracy, they nonetheless perceived the statements that rhymed as more accurate than those that didn't.

P5   The researchers explained that the rhyming phrases are characterized by greater processing fluency: They're mentally processed more easily than nonrhyming phrases. Because people tend to base accuracy evaluations, at least partly, on the perceived fluency of the incoming information, the rhyming statements are actually judged as more accurate. [72]

P6   These findings have many applications in everyday life. For one, the results of this research suggest that when marketers and business operators think about what slogans, mottos, trademarks, and jingles to employ, they should consider that using rhymes may increase not only the likability of the message, but also its perceived truthfulness. Perhaps this is why, when asked what a company could say about its product when there was nothing new to say about it, a seasoned advertising executive replied, "Well, if you have nothing to say about your product, then I suppose you can always sing about it."

P7   Second, parents can use rhyme to their advantage when faced with a common and frustrating influence challenge – getting their kids to go to bed. After quality time reading nursery rhymes with then, perhaps having them join in a few verses of "It's off to bed for sleepyhead" will prove persuasive.

P8   Finally, the power of rhyme can even be applied in a legal setting. In fact, the authors of this research point out one infamous rhyme that seems so weighty that it just may have tipped the scales of justice. During O.J. Simpson's murder trial, Johnnie Cochran, Simpson's defense attorney, told the jury, "If the gloves don't fit, you must acquit!" Considering the subtle influence of rhyme, the study's authors may be right to question how the verdict might have been affected if Cochran had instead implored, "If the gloves don't fit, you must find him not guilty!"

Goldstein, Noah J., Martin, Steve J., & Cialdini, Robert B. (2008) *Yes! 50 Scientifically Proven Ways to Be Persuasive*. New York: Free Press, pp.164-166.

Our journey exploring argument design, from the perspective of invention, organisation and style, is almost over. I hope the synthesis of Aristotelian rhetoric and contemporary linguistics has provided you with a dynamic framework for investigating the endlessly

---

[72] McGlone, M.S. and Tofighbakhsh, J. (2000) Birds of a feather flock conjointly (?): rhyme as reason in aphorisms. *Psychological Science*, 11:424-28.

fascinating ways in which we adapt our language use to effect change in the world by influencing our own and others' beliefs, attitudes and behaviour.

As with any skill, mastering rhetorical analysis takes practice and patience. The good news is that there is a vast archive of persuasion discourse, spoken, written and audiovisual, that you can access with the click of a mouse on the worldwide web. And, of course, there are our own daily encounters with a variety of individuals and groups, in formal and informal settings, in public, private and/or technical spheres, whether face-to-face or in cyberspace. Keep in mind the rule of three comprising text, subtext and context, as you scrutinise how rhetors adaptively employ the resources of language at the level of rhetorical structure, coherence relations and lexico-grammar to appeal to hearts, minds and character. And, you should be well on your way. Oh yes, and remember to have fun!

References

Birnbaum, Michael H. (1999). How to show that 9>221: Collect judgments in a between subjects design. *Psychological Methods, 4*(3), 243-249.

Booth, Wayne C. (1961). *The Rhetoric of Fiction.* Chicago: University of Chicago Press.

Booth, Wayne C. and Gregory, Marshall W. (1991). *The Harper & Row rhetoric: Writing as thinking and thinking as writing* (2nd edition) New York: HarperCollins.

Brinton, A. (1985). A rhetorical view of the ad hominem. *Australasian Journal of Philosophy* 65, 50-63.

Bruner, Jerome S. (1957) On perceptual readiness. *Psychological Review, 64*(2), 123-152.

Campbell, Karlyn K. and Huxman, Susan S. (2009). *The Rhetorical Act: Thinking, speaking and writing critically* (4th edition). Belmont, CA: Wadsworth Cengage Learning.

Ede, Lisa, and Andrea Lunsford. (1984). Audience Addressed/Audience Invoked: The Role of Audience in Composition Theory and Pedagogy. *College Composition and Communication 35*(2): 155-71.

Fairhurst, Gail T. (2005). Reframing the art of framing: Problems and prospects for leadership. *Leadership 1*(2), 165-185.

Gibson, Walker. (1950). Authors, Speakers, Readers, and Mock Readers. *College English 11*(5), 265-69.

Goldstein, Noah J., Martin, Steve J., and Cialdini, Robert B. (2008) *Yes! 50 Scientifically Proven Ways to Be Persuasive.* New York: Free Press, pp.164-166.

Hymes, Dell. (1972). Models of the interaction of language and social life. In J. Gumperz and D. Hymes (Eds.), *Directions in Sociolinguistics: The ethnography of communication.* New York: Holt, Rinehart & Winston, pp.35-71.

Keren, Gideon. (2011). On the definition and possible underpinnings of framing effects: a brief review and a critical evaluation. In G. Keren (Ed.) *Perspectives on Framing.* New York & Hove: Psychology Press, pp.3-33.

Leff, Michael. (2003). Rhetoric and Dialectic in Martin Luther King's 'Letter from Birmingham Jail'. In Frans H. van Eemeren, J. Anthony Blair, Charles A. Willard and A. Francisca Snoeck Henkemans (Eds.), *Anyone Who Has a View: Theoretical contributions to the study of argumentation*. Dordrecht: Kluwer Academic Publishers, pp. 255-268.

Levin, Irwin P., Schneider, Sandra L. and Gaeth, Gary J. (1998). All frames are not created equal: A typology and critical analysis of framing effects. *Organizational Behavior and Human Decision Processes, 76*(2) 149-188.

Mills, Harry. (2000). *Artful Persuasion: How to command attention, change minds, and influence people.* New York: AMACOM.

Preston, John. (1970) *The Created Self: The Reader's Role in Eighteenth-Century Fiction.* London: Heinemann.

Sherbo, Arthur. (1969), *Studies in the Eighteenth Century English Novel.* East Lansing: Michigan State University Press.

Swales, John. (1990). *Genre Analysis: English in academic and research settings*. Cambridge: Cambridge University Press.

Tversky, Amos and Kahneman, Daniel. (1981). The framing of decisions and the psychology of choice. *Science 211*(4481), 455-458.

van Buiten, Marc & Keren, Gideon. (2009) Speaker-listener compatibility: Joint and separate processing in risky choice framing. *Organizational Behavior and Human Decision Processes 108*(1), 106-115.

Works Cited

Aristotle. *The Art of Rhetoric.* (1991). Translated with an introduction and notes by Hugo Lawson-Tancred. Harmondsworth: Penguin Classics.

Atkinson, Max. (2004). *Lend Me Your Ears: All you need to know about making speeches and presentations.* London: Vermilion.

Austin, John L. (1962). *How To Do Things With Words.* New York: Oxford University Press.

Bazerman, Charles. (1988). *Shaping Written Knowledge: The genre and activity of the experimental article in science.* Madison: University of Wisconsin Press.

Bazerman, Charles. (1997). The life of genre, the life in the classroom. In W. Bishop and H. Ostrum (Eds.) *Genre and Writing.* Portsmouth, NH: Boynton/Cook, pp. 19-26.

Beardsley, Monroe C. (1970). *The Possibility of Criticism.* Detroit: Wayne State University.

Belcher, Diane. (1997). An Argument for non-adversarial argumentation: On the relevance of the feminist critique of academic discourse to L2 writing pedagogy. *Journal of Second Language Writing* 6(1), pp.1-21.

Birnbaum, Michael H. (1999). How to show that 9>221: Collect judgments in a between subjects design. *Psychological Methods,* 4(3) 243-249.

Booth, Wayne C. and Gregory, Marshall W. (1991). *The Harper & Row rhetoric: Writing as thinking and thinking as writing* (2nd edition) New York: HarperCollins.

Booth, Wayne C. (1961). *The Rhetoric of Fiction.* Chicago: University of Chicago Press.

Booth, Wayne C. (2005). Blind skepticism versus a rhetoric of assent. *College English,* 67(4), 378–388.

Bostrom, Robert N. (1983). *Persuasion.* Englewood Cliffs, NJ: Prentice-Hall.

Brinton, A. (1985). A rhetorical view of the ad hominem. *Australasian Journal of Philosophy* 65, 50-63.

Brockriede, Wayne. (1975/1990). Where is argument? In R. Trapp & J. Schuetz (Eds.) *Perspectives on Argumentation: Essays in honor of Wayne Brockriede.* Illinois: Waveland Press, pp.4-8.

Brown, Penelope and Levinson, Stephen C. (1987). *Politeness: Some universals in language use.* Cambridge: Cambridge University Press.

Bruner, Jerome S. (1957). On perceptual readiness. *Psychological Review,* 64(2), 123-152.

Campbell, Karlyn K. and Huxman, Susan S. (2009). *The Rhetorical Act: Thinking, speaking and writing critically* (4th edition). Belmont, CA: Wadsworth Cengage Learning.

Chapman, Graham, Idle, Eric, Gilliam, Terry and Jones, Terry. (1999). *Monty Python's Flying Circus Vol. 2.* London: Methuen.

Clifton, Jonathan and van de Mieroop, Dorien. (2010). 'Doing' ethos—A discursive approach to the strategic deployment and negotiation of identities in meetings. *Journal of Pragmatics 42,* 2449-2461.

Connor, Ulla. (1996). *Contrastive rhetoric: Cross-cultural aspects of second-language writing.* Cambridge, UK: Cambridge University Press.

Creme, Phyllis and Lea, Mary R. (2008). *Writing at university: A guide for students* (3rd edition). Open University Press (McGraw Hill).

Crider, Scott F. (2005). *The Office of Assertion: An art of rhetoric for the academic essay.* Wilmington, Delaware: ISI Books.

Ede, Lisa, and Andrea Lunsford. (1984). Audience Addressed/Audience Invoked: The Role of Audience in Composition Theory and Pedagogy. *College Composition and Communication 35*(2), 155-71.

Elbow, Peter. (2005). Bringing the rhetoric of assent and the believing game together—and into the classroom. *College English, 67*(4), 388–399.

Encyclopaedia Britannica. Retrieved on June 8, 2011 from http://www.britannica.com/EBchecked/topic/453093/persuasion.

Fairhurst, Gail T. (2005) Reframing the art of framing: Problems and prospects for leadership. *Leadership 1*(2), 165-185.

Feynman, Richard. (1955/1999). The Value of Science. In Robbins, J. (Ed.) *The pleasure of finding things out: the best short works of Richard P. Feynman.* Cambridge, MA: Perseus, pp. 141-150.

Gibson, Walker. (1950). Authors, Speakers, Readers, and Mock Readers. *College English 11*(5), 265-69.

Goffman, Erving. (1967). *Interaction Ritual: Essays on face-to-face behavior.* Allen Lane: The Penguin Press.

Goffman, Erving (1981). *Forms of Talk*. Philadelphia: University of Pennsylvania Press.

Gottman, John Mordecai. (1994). *What Predicts Divorce?* Hillsdale, NJ: Lawrence Erlbaum Associates.

Goodnight, Thomas. (1982). The personal, technical and public spheres of argument: a speculative inquiry into the art of public deliberation. *Journal of American Forensic Association 18*, 214-227.

Grice, H. Paul (1975). Logic and Conversation. In P. Cole and James L. Morgan (eds.) *Syntax and Semantics (vol.3) Speech Acts.* New York & London: Academic Press, pp.41-58.

Hairston, Maxine. (1976). Carl Rogers's Alternative to Traditional Rhetoric. *College Composition and Communication 27*(4), 373-377.

Halliday, Michael and Hasan, Ruqaiya. (1976). *Cohesion in English*. London: Longman.

Hinds, John (1983). Contrastive Rhetoric: Japanese and English. *Text 3*(2), 183-195.

Hoey, Michael (1983). *On the Surface of Discourse*. London: Allen & Unwin.

Hollihan, Thomas A. and Baaske, Kevin T. (2005). *Arguments and Arguing* (2nd edition) Long Grove, Illinois: Waveland Press.

Hymes, Dell. (1972). Models of the interaction of language and social life. In J. Gumperz and D. Hymes (Eds.), *Directions in Sociolinguistics: The ethnography of communication.* New York: Holt, Rinehart & Winston, pp.35-71.

Inch, Edward S. and Warnick, Barbara. (2010). *Critical Thinking and Communication: The use of reason in argument* (6th edition). Boston: Allyn & Bacon.

Jackson, Sally and Jacobs, Scott. (1980). Structure of Conversational Argument: Pragmatic Bases for the Enythmeme. *Quarterly Journal of Speech 66*(3), 251-265.

Jacobs, Scott and Jackson, Scott. (1982). Conversational argument: A discourse analytic approach. In J.R. Cox and C.A Willard (Eds.) *Advances in Argumentation Theory and Research.* Southern Illinois University Press.

Kaplan, Robert (1966). Cultural Thought Patterns in Intercultural Education. *Language Learning 16*(1-2), 1-20.

Keren, Gideon. (2011). On the definition and possible underpinnings of framing effects: a brief review and a critical evaluation. In Gideon Keren (Ed.) *Perspectives on Framing.* New York & Hove: Psychology Press, pp.3-33.

Lakoff, George and Johnson, Mark. (1981). *Metaphors we Live By.* Chicago: The University of Chicago Press.

Lanham, Richard A. (2003). *Analyzing Prose* (2nd edition) London: Continuum.

Latour, Bruno and Woolgar, Steve. (1986). *Laboratory Life: The Social Construction of Scientific Facts.* Princeton University Press.

Lawson-Tancred, Hugo. (Trans.). (1991). *The Art of Rhetoric.* Harmondsworth: Penguin Classics, pp.1-58.

Leff, Michael. (2003). Rhetoric and Dialectic in Martin Luther King's 'Letter from Birmingham Jail'. In Frans H. van Eemeren, J. Anthony Blair, Charles A. Willard and A. Francisca Snoeck Henkemans (Eds.), *Anyone Who Has a View: Theoretical contributions to the study of argumentation.* Dordrecht: Kluwer Academic Publishers, pp. 255-268.

Levin, Irwin P., Schneider, Sandra L. and Gaeth, Gary J. (1998). All frames are not created equal: A typology and critical analysis of framing effects. *Organizational Behavior and Human Decision Processes 76*(2), 149-188.

Lunsford, Andrea. (1979). Aristotelian vs. Rogerian argument A reassessment. *College Composition and Communication 30* (2), 146-151.

Lutz, William. (1996). *The New Doublespeak: Why no one knows what anyone's saying anymore.* HarperCollins.

Martin, James R. (1985). Process and text: Two aspects of human semiosis. In J.D. Benson & W.S. Greaves (Eds.) *Systemic Perspectives in Discourse, Vol. 1* Norwood, NJ: Ablex, pp.248-274.

Maslow, Abraham. (1943). A theory of human motivation. *Psychological Review 50*(4), 370-96.

Mauk, John. (2006). *Inventing Arguments.* Boston: Wadsworth Cengage Learning.

McDonald, Daniel. (1993). *The Language of Argument* (7th edition). New York: HarperCollins College Publishers.

Miller, Carolyn R. (1984). Genre as social action. *Quarterly Journal of Speech 70*, 151-167.

Mills, Harry. (2000). *Artful Persuasion: How to command attention, change minds, and influence people.* New York: AMACOM.

O'Keefe, Daniel. (1977). Two Concepts of Argument. *The Journal of the American Forensic Association* Vol. XIII, No. 3, 121-128.

Perelman, Chaim & Olbrechts-Tyteca, Lucie. (1969). *The New Rhetoric: A Treatise on Argumentation.* Trans. J Wilkinson & P. Weaver. Notre Dame: University of Notre Dame Press.

Polya, George. (1954). *Mathematics and Plausible Reasoning, Volume I: Induction and Analogy in Mathematics.* Princeton University Press.

Preston, John. (1970). *The Created Self: The Reader's Role in Eighteenth-Century Fiction.* London: Heinemann.

Ramage, John and Bean, John (1995). *Writing Arguments: A rhetoric with readings* (3rd edition) Boston: Allyn & Bacon.

Ramage, John, Bean, John and Johnson, June. (2010). *Writing Arguments: A rhetoric with readings* (8th ed.). New York: Longman.

Rieke, Richard D. and Sillars, Malcolm O. (2001). *Argumentation and Critical Decision Making* (5th ed.) New York: Longman.

Rogers, Carl. (1961). Communication: Its blocking and its facilitation. *On becoming a person* (pp. 27–34). New York: Houghton.

Rokeach, Milton. (1968). *Beliefs, Attitudes, and Values*. San Francisco: Jossey-Bass.

Rokeach, Milton. (1973). *The Nature of Human Values*. San Francisco: Free Press.

Schryer, Catherine F. (1993). Records as Genre. *Written Communication 10*(2), 200-234.

Searle, John R. (1976). The classification of illocutionary acts. *Language in Society 5*(1), 1-24.

Selzer, John. (2004). Rhetorical analysis: Understanding how texts persuade readers. In C. Bazerman & P. Prior (Eds.) *What Writing Does and How it Does it: An introduction to analysing texts and textual practices*. NJ: Lawrence Erlbaum, pp.279-307.

Sherbo, Arthur. (1969). *Studies in the Eighteenth Century English Novel*. East Lansing: Michigan State University Press.

Sutherland, Rory (2009). Life Lessons from an Ad Man. Ted Talk. Retrieved June 14, 2011, from http://www.ted.com/talks/lang/eng/rory_sutherland_life_lessons_from_an_ad_man.html

Swales, John. (1990). *Genre Analysis: English in academic and research settings*. Cambridge: Cambridge University Press.

Tannen, Deborah. (1998). *The Argument Culture: Moving from debate to dialogue*. New York: Random House.

Tannen, Deborah. (2002). Agonism in academic discourse. *Journal of Pragmatics 34*, 1651-1669.

Tubbs, Stewart L. (1968). Explicit versus implicit conclusions and audience commitment. *Speech Monographs 35* (1), pp. 14-19.

Tversky, Amos and Kahneman, Daniel. (1981). The framing of decisions and the psychology of choice. *Science 211*(4481), 455-458.

van Buiten, Marc and Keren, Gideon. (2009). Speaker-listener compatibility: Joint and separate processing in risky choice framing. *Organizational Behavior and Human Decision Processes 108*(1), 106-115.

van Eemeren, Frans H. and Grootendorst, Rob. (2004). *A systematic theory of argumentation: the pragma-dialectical approach*. Cambridge University Press.

Weaver, Richard M. (1953). Ultimate Terms in Contemporary Rhetoric. *The Ethics of Rhetoric*. Chicago: H. Regnery, pp. 212-32.

Wenzel, Joseph. (1990). Three Perspectives on Argument: Rhetoric, Dialectic, Logic. In R. Trapp & J. Schuetz (Eds.) *Perspectives on Argumentation: Essays in honor of Wayne Brockriede*. Illinois: Waveland Press, pp.9-26.

Wittgenstein, Ludwig. (1958). *Philosophical Investigations*. Oxford: Basil Blackwell.

Young, Richard E., Becker Alton L. and Pike, Kenneth L. (1970). *Rhetoric: Discovery and change*. New York: Harcourt, Brace and World.

Ziegelmueller, George W. and Kay, Jack. (1997). *Argumentation: inquiry and advocacy* (3rd edition). Boston: Allyn and Bacon.